BEYOND AMBITION

Mr Banks & Mr Kika

First version printed in Pretoria, 2019

Updated version, Copyright © 2022

ISBN: 978-0620-85294-4

Mr Banks (Author)

Talifhani Mamafha   - LinkedIn
atmamafha@gmail.com
@mrbanks_aa
www.analyticsadvert.com
081 709 0709

Mr Kika (Author)

Xolani Gule   - LinkedIn
bookssalmon@gmail.com
@kika_redefined
Salmon Publishers - (FB & IG)
065 846 6190

Donald Ntuli (Cover & Artwork)

Phakamani Design Studios
Pkay.trump@gmail.com
064 336 9493

Contents

-PREFACE-

Writing this book is to us a predestined service. In the following pages we unpack my business model and personal philosophy. I cannot medically confirm that I'm dyslexic, but I do have dyslexic tendencies as a result I compensate this condition with hiring the best of the best in trades and industries.

To pen this book, I knew I needed to find a spiritual person, an ordained pastor with life experience to translate my mind, spirit and calling.

After completing matric, I went to study Statistics at the University of Pretoria (UP) between 2009-2012. If you think I've never failed, you've got it all wrong. I've failed beyond numbers. I've been in lofty debts, and I've been heavily broke, but I never stopped grinding for my ambition to grow into a successful CEO of a leading innovative company. When you come from the bottom like us, you don't expect handouts or favours. The goal is to go beyond normal in building a world class business and brands. This book is testament that you can't add value in places you don't belong.

In reading this book it's important for you to understand that our success is not microwaved and nor is it based on an overnight success phenomenon. We've paid in full. Our aim is to preach impact, long term investment and value in helping others.

Pastor Kika and I first met physically in Rosebank, 130 Oxford Road. He came to my office, our energies aligned, and we spiritually connected. He had on a copy of his then recent book, 'The Unemployables', prefaced by Mr Seth Mazibuko, a 1976 June 16 Student Leader who was imprisoned in Robben Island at the age of 16.

In the book Kika writes about a group of young men and women who decides to CREATE their own OPPORTUNITIES instead of complaining about the government, unemployment and poverty. His views on society, morality and business confirmed our divine connection. His scope of study ranges from Economics, Theology, Creative Writing and TV & Film Production, for the latter course he graduated in 2018 from Tshwane University of Technology (TUT). He currently works as a publishing and film executive.

As we write, Analytics Advertising is a 4X award winning company with international clients and contracts from leading industries. In 2017 I left a 45K monthly salary to build an innovative multi-million-rand corporation within 4 years. Today, we're the tt100 Business Innovative Awards winner in the Management of Technology, Management of Innovation, Management of People and the Department of Science & Innovation's minister award for Overall Excellence as a medium size enterprise.

Salmon Publishers has worked on books from renowned celebrities and passionate professionals with significant stories to tell, stories that frequently appear on traditional and modern media platforms. Kika is a force behind many listed books, a maestro in creative writing with 10 years' experience in publishing. In this book, we share with you the BLUEPRINT to greatness, a strategy that worked, BEYOND AMBITION!

1.

$$x_{1,2} = \frac{-b \pm \sqrt{D}}{2a}$$

$$z = \frac{1}{x}$$

$$a^2 = b^2 + c^2 - 2 \cdot \frac{a}{2}$$

$$z = \frac{1}{x}$$

$$E^2 \quad p^2 = m^2 a$$

$$\frac{a}{\sin \alpha} = \frac{b}{\sin \beta} = \frac{c}{\sin \gamma}$$

$$\frac{2x}{x^2 + 2y^2} = 2$$

$$E = mc^2$$

The Crave

$$C = \begin{pmatrix} 0,1 \\ 1,0 \end{pmatrix}$$

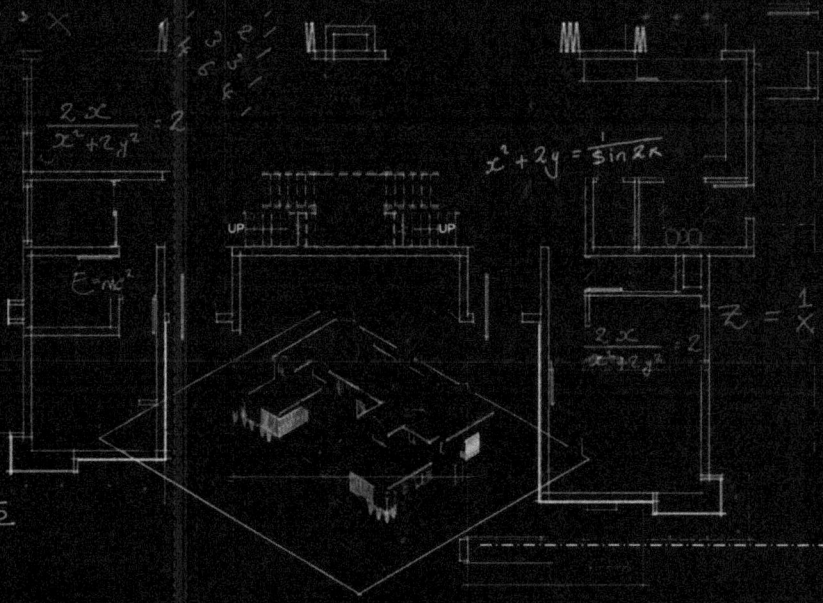

$$x_{1,2} = \frac{-b \pm \sqrt{D}}{2a}$$

$$\frac{2x}{x^2 + 2y^2} = 2$$

$$x^2 + 2y = \frac{1}{\sin 2x}$$

$$E = mc^2$$

$$z = \frac{1}{x}$$

$$\frac{2x}{x^2 + 2y^2} = 2$$

$$x_{1,2} = \frac{-b \pm \sqrt{D}}{2a}$$

Built-in For Business

"You can't add value in places you don't belong.
I was never comfortable working for corporate"

Growing up in Louis Trichardt was an amazing experience, we had nothing to worry about except eating, playing soccer and swimming. To this day I still have brilliant swimming moves and soccer skills, skills I acquired in Makhado.

I had faith in my plans and what I was going to do in the future. I almost dropped out of high school; I knew what I wanted to do but let's agree it would have been hard without University Knowledge to achieve what I had in my thoughts. My current business needs both school of thoughts, informal and formal education.

After completing matric, I went to study Statistics at the University of Pretoria (UP), between 2009-2012. I will not lie I had a wonderful opportunity to study in one of the best Universities and work for the best companies in South Africa.

I worked as a Pricing Analyst, Lecturer, and a Business Analyst. I founded "Analytics Advertising" with the aim to become the industry leader for breeding amazing brands by simply combining Strategy, Analytics, Creativity, brand associations and Strong communication skills.

I left what most people would call a decent job to answer my calling and fulfil the burning desire inside. I am not a vision maintainer; I am a visionary and a pioneer. I associate myself with people who not only value my energy but value my strategies and solutions.

Everything I had planned for my life was in schedule and in check. At the age of 19 I completed my matric and by the age of 23 I graduated from the University of Pretoria in BCom Statistics (Econometrics). I was a C student; I knew what to do to obtain required results.

I had my share of applying for jobs and spending time on Pnet, but I cannot say I struggled that much to get my first job. I found a job in one of the biggest retail companies in South Africa as a private brands analyst for a year. I then went to teach Statistics and Economics at Damelin College for 6 months then moved back to another best retailer as a Pricing Analyst. Everything was going according to plan and the future looked bright.

One day in 2016, I sat alone and asked myself tough questions about my life: With all that I have achieved, why am I still unhappy? What is it with me that keeps losing interest in climbing the corporate ladder? What is it that I want?

I wanted more; I wasn't happy with the status quo. I wanted a life more than just staying afloat and paying bills. I craved for something bigger. Ideally, I wanted to make a difference in society. It was inevitable for me to start my own company even when I was a very effective employee. Not that there was anything wrong with my employers, I just couldn't picture myself as an employee for the rest of my life.

I drafted my resignation letter and carried it to work. The manager, a lady I respected and preferred to talk to before handing in the letter was not around that day, so I kept it. I've been coming with it to work every day for 2-months, I think I wasn't ready then. I destroyed the letter and completely forgot about *the crave*.

My next manager was my employer, he made his plans for me in the company very clear. I really loved and respected his leadership and faith in me. I knew then that there was nothing more for me to do there except to idle around the office waiting for payday.

My mind was already out and swimming with sharks – Mr Banks

I decided to write an email to both my manager and HR, the HR manager saw the email first and called me, she was really surprised. That was the first time I jumped off the cliff, I didn't know if I was going to survive in business, but I trusted and believed.

After some time, I received a call to consult at automotive industry and because I was still thinking about safety mentally and I had all the requirements and responsibilities, I fell for it. They paid me about 45K monthly, I was sorted and doing well. After few months, the craving came back stronger. It was clear I was called for something greater and had to respond accordingly.

This was beyond making money or becoming wealthy. I think many of my peers still take it wrong, they look at me and think I just love money which I do, or I just want to be seen or I just talk too much. They couldn't to this day understand the fire burning inside of me, the purpose I had to carry through.

It's always funny when you explain this because people who don't have this in them don't understand. I don't think they will ever understand until they are called into something greater than their perspective of life. It's hard to explain these things to short-minded people who'd rejoice in imagining what they can do with 45K on a monthly basis, nothing more.

It's not for the theorists but the doers – Mr Banks

Finally, I was ready to leave everything and start a new life. I always thank God for my supportive wife "Paby", she has been and still is my pillar of strength. She can tell you everything about my worst days. Some days I'd be so discouraged and feel like I didn't deserve to eat, she'll dish up for me and respectfully hand me my food after a long unproductive day. Some days were better than others.

I jumped at opportunities and took all possible risks, some paid off and some I count as losses, it's part of the game, you win some and you lose some. Some of the decisions I made seemed unsuccessful at first but later proved my intelligence. I still remember how we invested all our money and energy in the business, which struggled to pull through in its earlier days. Many small businesses operate on 'survival mode', aiming for break-through success. We remained consistent and relevant in providing solutions to our clients and customers, by so doing we became a success story.

Before this status, it was easy and tempting to give up, the best thing to do for me was to update my CV and go back to corporate. I knew that I had more to offer and so I endured all critics and temptations. Like any start-up, we worked hard at first for it to pick up. So, I put my CV aside and pursued my dream.

Waking up every day knowing very well that your mind is elsewhere, and you're no longer interested in what you're doing can be challenging. You're not adding value, constantly doing the same thing as a machine was a complete struggle for me. As hard as it was, I left my comfort zone. The retail guru, Raymond Ackerman puts it this way:

"I never thought of myself as an entrepreneur. If I had not been fired from what I thought was a secure job in a large corporation, I would never have started my own business. Now it seems inconceivable that I might have been an employee in my entire life, but I may very well have been seduced by the comforts of a steady income and company benefits".

My kind of people, disruptors, are always up for challenges and different things. We don't enjoy doing the same thing every day. We want change, spontaneity and innovation. I wanted to live and act according to my ideas and dreams. Some people take us lightly, I guess that's how you become great when you begin to do the impossible.

> "After many unsuccessful attempts to get my book published, I decided to start my own publishing company. I've always believed that if they can't give you what you deserve, just start your own. For example, if they can't record your first album, start your own studio. I have a bad case of Do-It-Yourself syndrome".

> -Mothibedi Moss Sereme, Drum magazine,
> 11/December/2014 issue.

Believe in yourself and trust in your abilities. My previous employer once sent me a text back when I was working in Sales that wrote: "Success is simple, fix your eyes on the prize and enjoy the ride".

There are two roads to choose from, the easy route (the one I prefer to call the universal route), and the road less travelled, (offers bigger secrets and challenges. However, just as she texted me, one must first identify the prize (goal) before enjoying the ride (journey), fear usually delights in the latter route (the road less travelled). There's neither fear nor struggle in doing what everyone is doing.

I have a disease called AMBITION success is the cure.
The only way I'll heal is when I SUCCEED – Mr Banks

Even when we tell you our stories, we cannot tell you HOW to succeed, you need to walk your own path. To this very day, we don't make excuses, we set pace and provide results in spite of field challenges. The sooner you stop blaming others for your responsibilities, the faster you can search and find opportunities to execute.

If you could ask us, why we wanted to succeed so badly our answer would probably rotate around the fact that we lived to hate poverty. We don't know what your definition of poverty is, but we believe poverty to be the inability to see ideas and opportunities.

People mistakenly think poverty is measured by what one has or do not have, we disagree. It is the way one thinks of himself that determines his state of liberty. In our understanding pessimists and mediocre are the poorest people in the world. Confidence is the name of the new game; your self-perception is as important as your business profile.

It bothers us to hear people say that they were born poor and therefore, cannot do anything about their situation whilst others (those who see their gift) utilize their skills and ideas for profit and gain (monetization). I mean that is an insult to God or should I say, The Creator because He never allowed the identification of man to be attached to materialistic possessions as we humans usually do. He gave every man character, skill, and talent.

It is our use of those given attributes that lead to most of us labelling ourselves poor in the face of the earth. Most of us were born in families with limited, if any resource, but amongst those, some have managed to accumulate wealth in all forms you can imagine, others are on the verge of living their dreams, whereas the rest, who believed in defining themselves poor or disadvantaged, remain so, but then again, who is to blame?

> 'Don't say you don't have enough time. You have exactly the number of hours per day that were given to Hellen Keller, Pasteur, Michaelangelo, Mother Teresa, Leonardo da Vinci, Thomas Jefferson & Albert Einstein.' - *H. Jackson Brown*

The sooner we realize that we become who we are by how we use our 24 hours and manage changes around us, we'll begin at once to execute our ideas. We, like Mr. Thakaruji and other examples mentioned later in the book have pestering dreams, dreams to breakout from the survival mode and merely living. We long to create long-lasting relationships with our customers and supporters, we want to rise in prominence as we help the less fortunate reach their full potential. Our aim is not only to make PROFIT but to IMPACT.

Above all, we discovered that there's no sweet success without OTHERS hence, millionaires don't live in desserts but in the city, where people can see and admire. And so, we realized that our value comes from the people we serve and certainly not from our egos and self. We joined heads and worked on a project that is BEYOND our AMBITIONS. To point out that much is owed to our families and society.

The thought of LEGACY has raced me to a point where I found myself re-drafting my resignation letter and breaking free from corporate claws and benefits. I first started by building brands (products and artists). Managing artists and dealing with individual clients was not an ideal way of doing business. I reinvented my company to do business with corporate, where my financial fate relies on an automated system and not human emotions. I learned that a person could agree to pay you on this day but change when the day comes due to circumstances, but a machine is reliable, no excuses, only results. Emotions can't get you this far, a reliable model and system will.

"

You can't add value in places you don't belong.

I was never comfortable working for corporate.

"

I have a disease called AMBITION success is the cure. The only way I'll heal is when I SUCCEED.

"

Emotions can't get you this far, a reliable model and system will.

2.

Make your

move

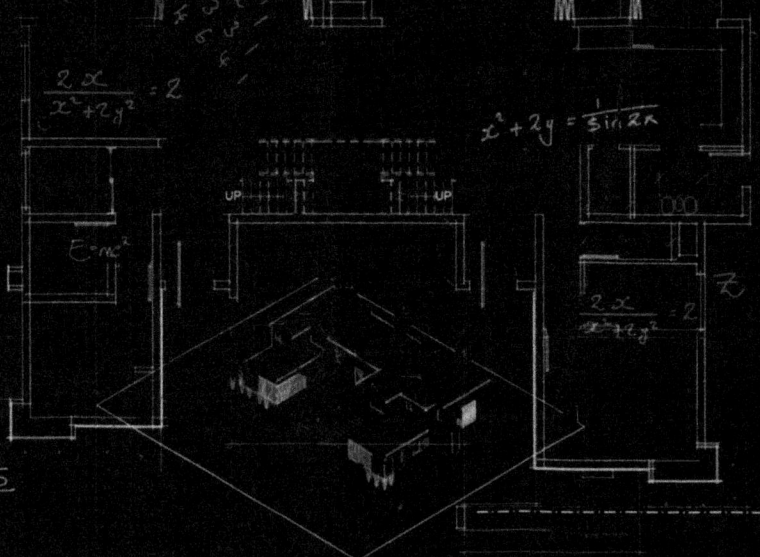

An ambitious young man asked an experienced salesman for the secret of his success in selling. The salesman said," There's no great secret, you just must jump at every opportunity that comes along." The young man replied, "But how can I tell when an opportunity is coming?" The salesman responded," You can't. You must keep jumping."

"A good man is always a beginner". Martial (c.40-c.104)

Life is about interactions; you can't live alone. We are social animals, and we connect by speaking and adding value to each other. It's good to receive something from someone and be thankful. As much as it takes guts to beg, we feel that is better than create and helping hence most people prefer to be on the receiving end, grants and tenders.

We all can change lives, the hand that gives is more blessed than the hand that receives, go where there's blessings, don't invite curses to your space.

It is more important to be a giver, you learn how to generate more and feed others, and you add value to your life when you solve someone's problems. Nobody will be remembered for begging, but many leaders who changed lives by giving something to the world will live forever.

You are only as valuable as what you give, if you give nothing, you do not ignite value. You get respect based on what you do and how you make an impact. Surprisingly, that's how every great person became a legend, you must give something for value. I had to build brands first for you to respect my work, she had to first put a great song out, and he had to write so many books to publish the right one. In any case, you must do the work, make your move.

You are a community of cells that sense energy, what I mean is you can easily sense where your energy function better, before you move, use your senses to understand the direction to take. Your cells communicate with you all the time; therefore meditation, prayer and relaxation are essential for humankind. Understand different vibrations and spend time where you add value and where you're valued. This alone will increase your belief in self and develop confidence in you to keep going. It's an ongoing process, is not a destination but a journey, you become better with time.

I worked with Moonchild Sanely from 2015 taking content and strategically helping her brand take off from the ground. We believed in what we were doing. It was a lot of time invested on one brand and other people as well. Looking at where her brand is right now you realize it takes consistency and belief in one's ability and the team around you. Otherwise, they wouldn't have created such materials that added value for you.

You learn to respect people and identify the relevant people to associate with to benefit the brand. Creativity comes in uncertainty, with experience you learn to operate outside your comfort zone, you focus on the next opportunity instead of wasting time talking about what you used to do.

Avoid the trap of LIVING IN YOUR PAST ACHIEVEMENTS.
Life goes on and so should you – Mr Kika

I worked on Mohale Motaung's brand, one of the biggest brands coming up. One of the few young, dedicated and inspirational personality I'd crossed paths with. We sit and strategize, develop and create materials that put the brand as a household brand. I am excited talking about such brands because one day people will look at it and say but how did you get here and realize its small steps done well which turned out to be a great value accumulated over time in the future.

You are only respected as the value you bring and the difference you make to others. South Africa (consuming country) is regarded as one of the most unequal societies in the world. In 2008, South Africa's Gini-coefficient reached an all-time high of 0, 7. Ten years later, there's still no positive change but the widening of the wealth gap.

Given our history as a Country, disadvantaged blacks, I can assure you that the lack of bread is not our main problem. Our main problem is seeing our dear brother with a bakery failing to share with those in grave need. We deeply believe that when one of us gets ahead, he or she must morally teach and reach others. The Black tax phenomenon is nothing but an offspring of such a mentality. Mind you, we're not condemning breaking bread with brothers, but we don't want you to suffer in expectation, we want you to make your move regardless of their actions.

Dr. Mukanda Mulemfo, in his book, Thabo Mbeki: *An African Renaissance Voice,* uses the following story to illustrate his argument on the African development and the pitiable PHD, Pull Him/Her Down Syndrome of which many of us are in fact infected or affected.

> There was once a man who went to heaven accidentally. Before he could enter the gates of heaven, he was kept in the waiting place by God's secretary awaiting his clearance

whether to go to heaven or hell. The waiting place was a warm place and there was also a lot of noise coming from the opposite direction. Then, he became curious and wanted to find out what was going on there. He looked around to find out where the noise was coming from, and he then saw a big pot full of people who were all unhappy and were jumping up and down trying to get out. What struck him was that only white people's heads were visible when they were jumping as they were trying to get out. All the time when a white head tried to rise-up, the security guard knocked it down with a baton back into the pot. Coming from a black majority country, he found it strange that he never saw a single Black head among those jumping since he was concerned about Black people. He approached the security guard and asked him, why are there only white people in the pot? The security guard answered with a question, why do you ask? The man said it is because I just saw that all the heads you were beating were only white. The security guard explained to him that there were also Black people in there, but they could not make it to the top because all the time when a Black person wants to go up, other Blacks pull him/her down.

(Mulemfo 2000:92)

I have this strong connection to people who inspire me, I know very well that we are different, we are described as crazy and stupid by people and that makes us different. When I was at university, I used to read about Steve Jobs, and I became more interested in his stories and YouTube videos. He was very inspiring, but the main thing was what he did better than most tech companies, which was marketing. I just knew how to sell.

On my final year I decided to attend marketing first year classes just to get more knowledge in Advertising. That part alone somehow shaped the man I am today. I like Steve's vision and ideas to develop a brand that became a movement to societies internationally.

Les Brown has been my motivator and the man I can rely on when it comes to inspiration. He talked about things that were relevant to me and real. It wasn't fiction or made-up stories, I could easily connect with him.

Jay Z has been my all-time favourite when it comes to music, entrepreneurship and lifestyle. I listened to his music over and over repeating after him until I would understand lyrics, word for word. I could understand what he was saying beyond entertainment, and I believe that's what got him where he is today. He is a powerful man by believing in himself and his abilities. He is open to ideas and new ways to do business. I connected with his story to this day.

Robert green - After reading 48 laws of Power, 50th law, Mastery and the law of Human Nature I just have to put him on the list. He is one of the best guys that helped shape my thinking. A lot of things that I didn't understand as clear as now that today it's part of a lifestyle. A lot of habits I had to change and how I look at myself from within. I learned that how I see the world is based on the content I have in me. Which made me realize not every good content is for me.

The food of content that can feed me well is his type of content. I learned so much from Robert Green I hope he understands how much he contributes to our lives. I am inspired by other musicians, business owners and philanthropists. Lastly, I will talk about Floyd Mayweather. I love his belief in self and the genius level talent in him. Coming from poverty people don't expect you to become much but as he became what he is, he attracted a lot of hate.

Some people don't expect you to be where you belong,
they just feel like you don't deserve it – Mr Banks

I like the fact that Floyd is confident and aware that such spirits are just there to hate his success and growth. He is a hard worker and he dedicated himself to the sport of boxing. I took that from him and his consistency in the sport. I learned that you don't have to be great today or strive to be the best only for today but to be consistent in winning.

There's no luck but WORK. People run around with witch doctors looking for answers, but the truth lies in consistency and self-belief. My philosophy about life is to take care of yourself, be mindful of the content you consume, be mindful of your environment or people you associate yourself with. To be a man or woman of wealth or poverty lies in your thoughts, content and your words. Believe in yourself and what you can do.

You don't have that luxury to wait for your friend to approve you, they also don't know you that well. Find yourself and project to the world who you are and after a while you will see us respond to you. You are part of the ecosystem of life. You will have associates, it's up to you who you choose to spend most of your time with. It is true as we've said before that your five friends determine where you are going in the coming years.

Never confuse your friends with acquaintances, some people should just be the people you know, that's all. Spend time with those who help you strive to be better and achieve better results. Some people behave like hyenas, they wait for you to do the job then they show up, they only show up to eat. You cannot associate yourself with such losers, they will affect your thinking.

People who dedicate their time to talk bad about others can talk bad about you too, you're not safe in that quadrant. I am very careful of the content I put in my mind, that's why I am writing this book today, to feed in positive thoughts and turn dreams into reality.

True SUCCESS can be ACHIEVED BY HELPING OTHERS – Mr Kika

We wish you the best in all your endeavours and we hope you discover yourself by reading this book. We wrote this book with you in mind. Make it your mission to tell your story and lead a life BEYOND AMBITION, a life where you not only think about YOU and YOURS but OTHERS.

We understand that the helpless and the hopeless rely on us to play our part in giving them a leg-up, not a hand-out. In this book, we saw a gap and an opportunity to help and CHANGE LIVES as opposed to only enriching ourselves. We believe in grasshoppers jumping in; we take the responsibility of being open-minded and helpful.

'The starting point of every idea is the working point'.
- Joel Eze (Nigeria) *Manual Of Champions*

The problem, they say, is the starting point, especially after a fall or a failed attempt. It's often easy to dream, pray, hope, wish and believe. It's the starting point that seems to be the problem. Where do I start? Perhaps, you may be asking yourself the same or a similar question. I agree, talking is fun, working is something else unless if you talk for a living, that should be fun. But still, even if that is the case, you still must put in the work.

I don't know the key to success, but the key to failure is trying to please everybody - Bill *Cosby*

Success is a human need. Everyone needs to succeed in one way or the other. From the early 1870's and before, people flocked from their native regions to come dig diamonds in South Africa. I think success should be added in the constitution, chapter 2 in the Bill of Rights as a human right. The freedom charter is equivocated and not precise.

The truth of the matter is there's a system for everything. For you to succeed, you must understand and become a disciple of success. Why do you think we have so many books and movies talking about success? 2 STEPS TO BEING RICH, MILLIONAIRE MINDSET, WHY WE WANT YOU TO BE A BILLIONAIRE or any success-related title. They discovered they're secret and now they're exercising it.

'I'm going to Jozi to search for opportunities', they say. Jozi, slang for Johannesburg is well known as THE CITY OF GOLD. Well-known artists, corporate employees and employers, business owners and more used this formula to succeed. The 'pack-your-bags' and go to Jozi formula. Today, the formula is not as strong as it was decades ago.

Perhaps employment is not the issue here, but success is. In your opinion, how do you think people succeed? Could it be luck? The effort they exert or it's merely by accident? Do you think they attract success? Or they simply apply the so-called secrets to success? Perhaps they went to school and applied the theory correctly. What do you think?

Either way the answer to this question could be a relief to some if not most of us. I still don't think there's an ultimate formula for success although various mechanisms work for different people in different ways at different times. Malcolm S. Forbes once said: "Success follows doing what you want to do. There is no other way to be successful."

Do you agree with Malcolm? I feel the need to add on what he said by saying: "Indeed success follows doing what you want; it gets much easier if what you want to do is what you are able to do." As I've mentioned in the previous paragraph that there's no such thing as a specific secret to success, but Robert Browning couldn't have been more right when he said,

> " The critical ingredient is getting off your butt and **doing something**, It's as simple as that. A lot of **people have ideas**, but there are few who decide to do something about them now. Not tomorrow. Not next week. But today, **the true entrepreneur is a doer, not a dreamer**".

What I discovered and wrote about in my third book, THE UNEMPLOYABLES is that our people just want to be owners and managers. They just want to be CEO's, directors and valuable people in society. They want to study in Cambridge, Harvard or Oxford. They intend to become Astronauts, to someday go to space and see the galaxy and leave us behind. They want to live in Sandton and have other houses overseas. If you try to reason with them, they immediately develop hate towards you. In their dreams, they drive super cars and live lavish. They have 5 to 6 qualifications in case one gets outdated. They believe they equally deserve what Arkad (Richest man in Babylon) has, if not more. Life gives you what you negotiate and work for, not what you think you deserve, MAKE YOUR MOVE.

Growing up I always had visions of becoming an entrepreneur. I kept telling everyone I will be running a business one day. In 2015, I started working with entertainment people. I would help them with brand strategy to get endorsement deals with my analytics skills. Around that time, I turned professional in trading analytics and advertising, so I opened a company. I just felt tired and demotivated at the office as a Business Analyst. I called my father and told him I'm about to quit, knowing me he thought it was a great idea. I called my wife and told her that I was about to notify the HR manager that I would be leaving – she said let's go!

I resigned and served my notice!

Avoid the trap of LIVING IN YOUR PAST ACHIEVEMENTS. Life goes on and so should you.

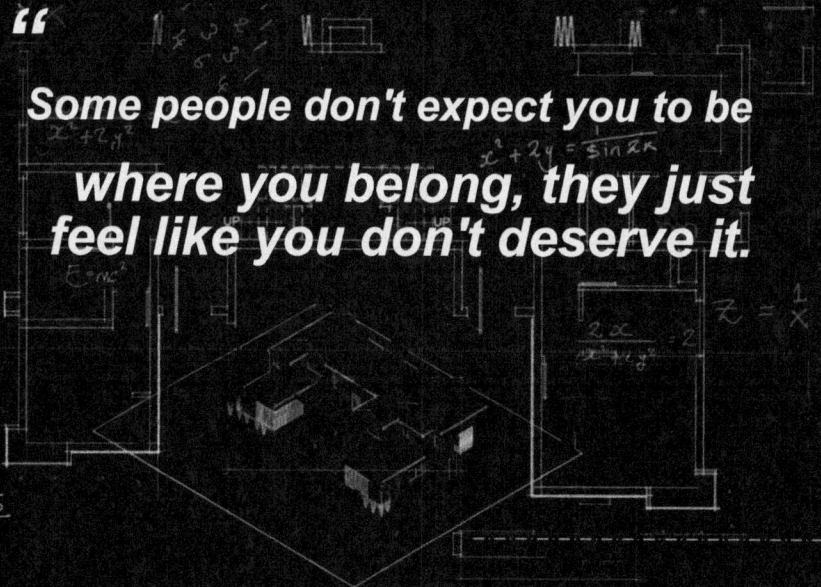

Some people don't expect you to be where you belong, they just feel like you don't deserve it.

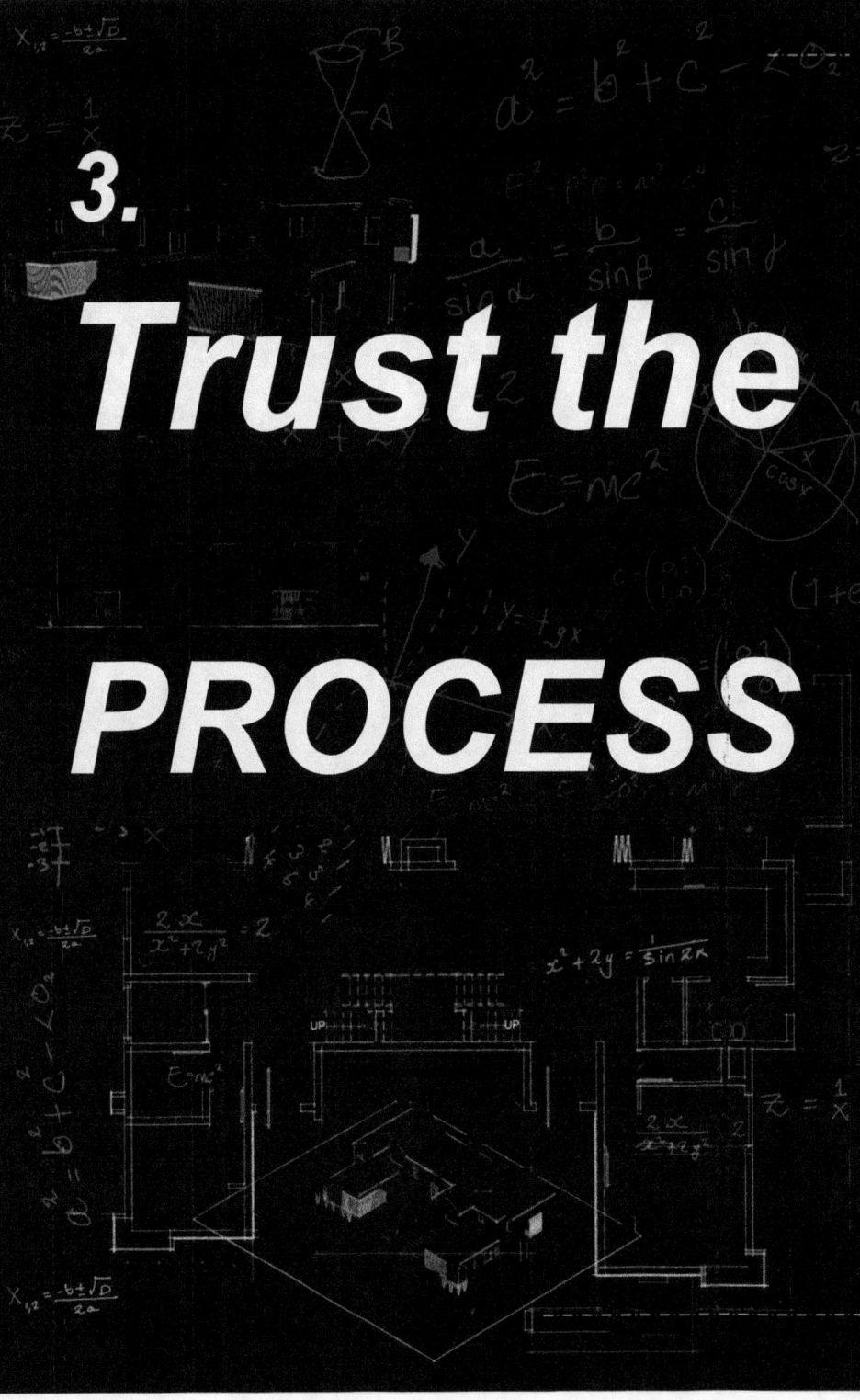

3.

Trust the

PROCESS

I named my son *Tyson*, after Tyson Fury, a British professional boxer, the Gypsy King, heavyweight champion. I admire his resilience and dedication to his craft. Many opponents often undermine him and that's how he knocks them down. Like warriors of 300, Tyson was born to fight and win.

Failure is part of the process; you can't grow without failure. As a pioneer nobody expects you to know everything. You are not inventing with a memorandum; you will constantly be required to refine your direction until you get it right. It takes time to build a powerful model that just connects to a level where everyone is interested to work with you. You will have to pass through some bridges and tunnels that will remind you that you're not on the right direction, but you were also required to pass through there. This is like having to unlock all the directionless doors to help you get to the right door. It's a heavy task and we appreciate it.

The people who don't win or who end up complaining about things being hard, usually give up on this stage. To us, this is the stage where you realize failure is part of success and as you fail it means you're growing and on a different level than yesterday. It also means the level you're on is unexpected.

Keep working and don't give up, you fail as you grow. We are on a different level now compared to when we started to write this book in 2019. We are on our fourth office, 240 square meter headquarters in Midrand. It's hard to talk about growth and success without failure. Today, we are here because of the mindset, you fail as you grow towards success.

Our biggest fear is not that we are inadequate, our biggest fear is that we are more powerful beyond measure.

The above quote comes from a book by Marianne Williamson called *A Return To Love*, we often attribute it to Nelson Mandela. I love this quote because it embodies the entire human truth in pursuing ones' purpose. Indeed, over the years fear has succeeded in killing many dreams and visions. Believing in yourself has emerged to being the leading cure of fear. The only fear we have is that of ourselves.

With everything that is said and done, fear will not go on a vacation, it will creep in at your worst moments. Like a persistent lawyer, it will persuade you to settle against your dream and drive. In the name of love and protection, at times fear will come to you in a form of family and friends. Your very own beloved will work hard to see you quit your dream with the intention of protecting you of course.

Your mind is like a garden, on that garden anything can grow. It doesn't take any courage for weeds to grow, it doesn't take any sunshine, any water, and weeds will still grow either way. Same with your mind, it doesn't take any courage for your mind to be negative, your mind is on automatic to be negative. At times to protect you, your brain sabotages you.

When you think negative things about yourself, you affect your self-esteem and confidence. You begin to question your abilities and worth, this alone leads to self-doubt, it's all in your mind. Fear kills dreams, stay hopeful and do not be afraid. Make your move and trust the process.

Train your mind to be less fearful, convince yourself that you are worthy, speak positive about yourself and enhance your esteem. Believe in yourself and your abilities. Start listing your small achievements to gain self-confidence. Be your own hype man, talk yourself not only into the game but also into winning. To win you must develop a winner's attitude, winners win, and losers lose.

Indeed, we are powerful beyond measure. Like the quote above, often we don't fear our inabilities but our power within. We understand that out of 100% of our creative brain capacity, we haven't utilized even a quarter that terrifies us especially when we imagine our full potential.

Evaluate and reshuffle your friends to those who represent where you are going. It's very important that you spend time with people who speak life in you, those who provide you with positive information and stuff that can build you to be your best. Your mind must get there before you.

Fear is an illusion that makes you lower your standards. Same situation can be presented positively if you change your mindset or have someone train your mind. Believe you are worthy; believe you are part of the ecosystem you wish to become part of. Don't only pray and fast for what you desire, like the re-builders of Jerusalem walls, build and fight, become a bricklayer and a protector of that building.

I feared that I might not have the ability to inspire people, I often questioned my right and license to speak to people and inspire them to become better. I used to question myself and undermine my strategy of communication. I listened to the great inspirational gurus like Zig Ziglar and felt discouraged. I didn't see myself fit for this responsibility little did I know that my style of communication is different and one of the best for my generation.

Success is a repetition of the process until value is added – Mr Banks

Today I speak in seminars, corporate trainings, meetings, schools and churches without fear. I believe in my story. I know every time after I speak, I lift a spirit. I specialize in fighting fear and his cousin doubt. I delight in shaking people from their sleep and I strongly believe in personal development and contributing to society.

Don't worship fear, oppress it until it ceases to exist in you. Do exactly that one thing you fear the most, things will change for the better. I can guarantee you all you need is persistence and consistency. Success is a repetition of the process until value is added. When a farmer plants a seed in the morning, he doesn't expect to see results in the evening, he does what he must and allows the process to take place without interference.

Any worthwhile GRIND and big idea take time, sometimes longer than expected. Colonel Sanders was 65 and on the verge of committing suicide, and at age 66 he founded and succeed in franchising KFC. Steve Harvey was 27 when his comedy business gained shape. Sean "Jay Z" Carter released his first album at age 26 and Ellen DeGeneres first appeared on the Johnny Carson Show at age 27. Even though age is relative, PATIENCE remains a virtue.

Mark Twain said at some point that "Age is an issue of mind over matter, if you don't mind, it doesn't matter". Peter Dinklage attained his acting debut at age 29 and Mike Epps gained his major comedy fame at age 27. Thomas Dexter, "Bishop TD Jakes" first appeared on TV at age 30.

Masaru Ibuka founded SONY at age 38, Henry Ford founded the Ford Motor Company at age 40 and Thomas Edison (former Henry Ford's employer), founded General Electric at age 43. Gordon Bowker founded Starbucks at age 51 and Adolf Dassler founded Adidas at age 49. My point here is, don't only see the glory, and understand the story. Be fast but never hurry, you will get there.

They don't want the process; they want the product – Mr Kika

Later in 2013, few months after I published my very first book "An Intelligent Fool", a young woman approached me and said, "It must be easy writing a book, I also want to write." Thoughts flooded my mind, I wanted to ignore her, her ignorance or rather naivety didn't sit well with me. The only reasonable thing that came out of my mouth was, "Believe me, writing a book is not as easy, simple, maybe" I said this to her as kind as possible.

The reality is, she's not alone, and many people believe it's that easy. They think you just rock up with ideas and write hence they say, "If you can do it, so can I". That's incorrect, you either can or can't. Many people have tried writing a book because they saw us writing but because they lack understanding of the craft, they often give up too soon.

I was gained experience working on various books and stories, Joel Eze (Nigeria) Tshepo Ditshego (Ekangala) Ps. J Mokgathlane (Soshanguve) L. Manyala (Vaal), the late Thabiso Khumalo (Teekay) my friend and illustrator and many others. I funded and published his very first comic book, Echo – Eric Powers in 2013 at the Pretoria State Theatre, Afro Lounge. His death left a void, we worked together in my corporation for some time, and he went to Mighty Media and later worked at Lemoko Group with Lebogang Mokhubela.

We don't want you to get over motivated and get the wrong idea, this is tough business. You must be fully in and committed, you must stay focused and consistent. This is serious, we've been betrayed, played and insulted. We felt the heat and endured the pain of loss and disappointment, it's part of the game.

Arkard lost his years' savings, time and youth pleasures to become the richest man in Babylon. He had to first expose crave to succeed by acting on his knowledge and desire. Robert Kiyosaki had to spend years failing in business and observing his two Dads to develop the concept of Rich Dad, Poor Dad, this is not just a book, but life experience summed up in solutions.

We share the same view and sentiment with *Robert Kiyosaki* in saying, to pursue your dream you must have a spine and do something about it (fear) instead. The fear of being different prevents most people from seeking new ways to solve their problems. Winners are not afraid of losing but losers are. Failure is part of the process of success. People who avoid failure also avoid success.

"

Success is a repetition of the process until value is added.

"

They don't want the process; they want the product.

4.
Too deep to QUIT

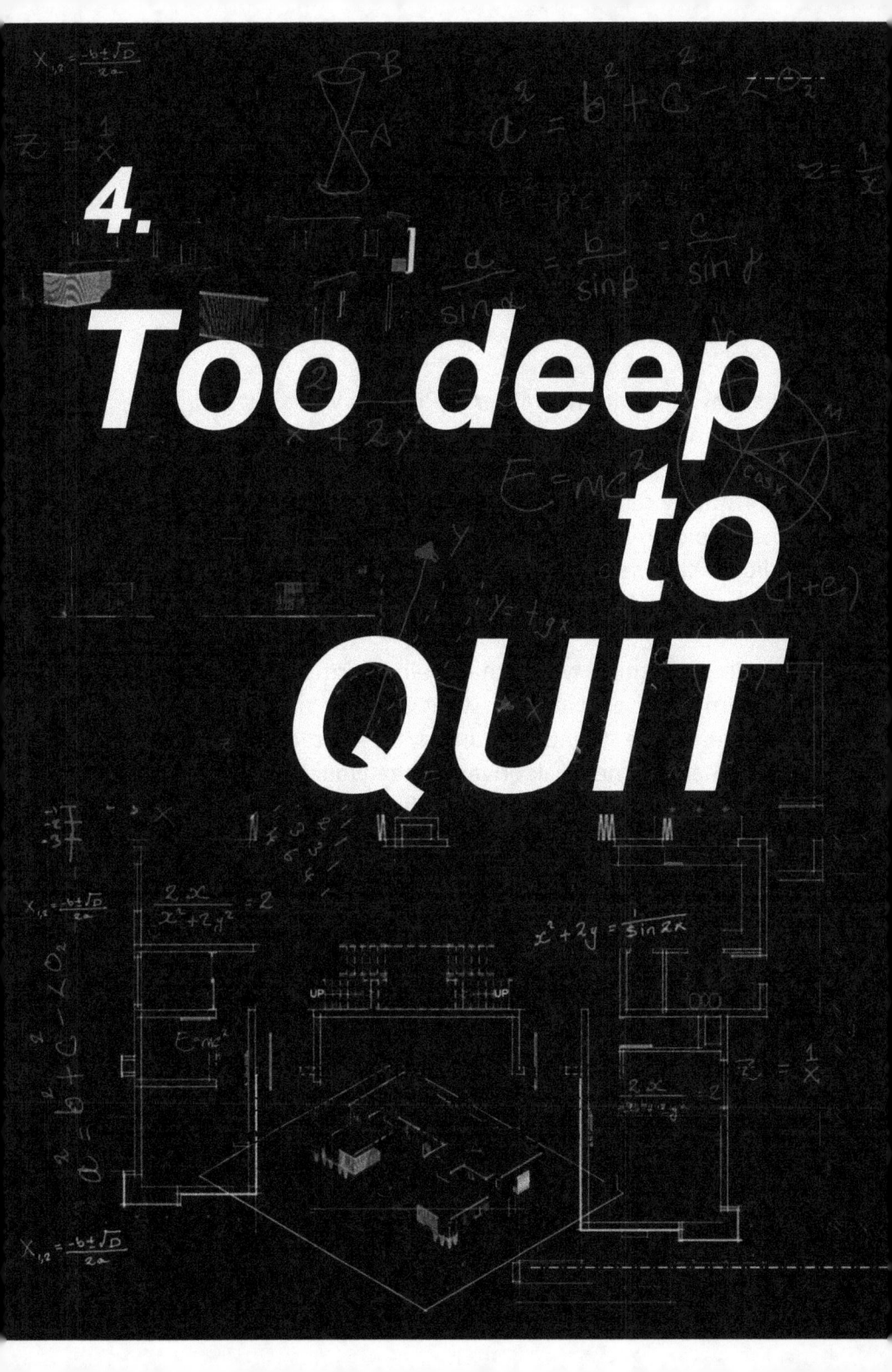

Sometimes it was hectic, some nights were better, and some days were the best. We had our share of poverty like any other impoverished black family, it wasn't easy at all especially when the poverty lasted longer. We believed every day that it will get better, we had ambitions and we listened to inspirational music to lift our spirits up, to dream even bigger.

I spent time with my father in Pretoria West, Atteridgeville. Life was simple and fun to those who loved and acclimatized to that environment. For someone like me, it wasn't as fun. I was constantly searching for an escape gate to get out of the hood, I never pictured myself living there for a long time. Even though I didn't stay for a longer period in Atteridgeville, it seemed longer.

There is nothing worse than being surrounded by people who dream small or who only want average things in life for their future. Some friends dreamed to be security guards, some police and some truck drivers. They would gladly explain to me how they are going to buy their first car, what model and which one makes sense and seem possible to achieve, that was not my kind of topics and vibe.

I felt like an outsider in a company of small dreamers – Mr Banks

For them, that was big achievements, not for me. I battled every day to get out of the hood, so I spent most of my time in the house, reading, and on the internet. I spent most of my money on airtime and data to connect with friends who think alike, big dreamers and inspirational personalities. That alone saved me from the street.

I knew exactly what I wanted, I used to read about business and spent my days in town doing things that sparked my brain to become better. The escape gate was employment at that time, the businesses we started couldn't last long, it was mainly because of lack of knowledge and some we blamed it on "no capital" but of course, it was lack of experience.

I began to work, did the inevitable and moved out of the hood. I'm growing and expecting to gain financial freedom yet at the back of my mind I know I am supposed to be working for myself. I kept that idea in mind, the craving grew to a point where I quit and started my business, Analytics Advertising. I've learned a lot in the business since I started. I've learned a lot about life and people, I paid attention to two major things, books and people. Find out what lazy and poor people read and don't dare read it.

My business used to be depressed often when I failed to close a deal or when my business is crumbling and when I couldn't pay rent and salaries. It was tough and painful. I paid my bond last after paying my employees, some months, I couldn't provide for my family. I learned over the years that it's very important to have a strong family that support by actions not merely by words or just looking at you. Not that there's anything wrong with prayer but I needed money then not prayers. It wasn't easy, some people looked at me like, you really think highly of yourself, we told him not to quit, and he thinks he is better than everyone else.

I received all of that, sometimes you have people who just don't believe in you at all, and like how do you think you can do that? How can you build a powerful brand? I think I had to learn to stop absorbing people's opinions. I began to focus on myself and what I think I could do; I focused every day on positivity and creating new things and ideas.

That method really added value to me. Everywhere I go now they say "Talifhani, you are doing great things"! Well, I don't see it yet, I don't think I'm there yet, but I've grown compared to where I come from. This is not easy, it is not for the timid and the theorist, it is for the doers and the fearless.

Like suicide, thinking about quitting is not a problem, the problem is the actual quitting – Mr Kika

I learned to believe in myself and what I can do over time when I saw the same people who were doubting my abilities asking for my services politely, that's when I knew they needed me. It takes time to build a strong, sustainable and reliable brand. It takes a lot from you. It's about the process and not necessarily the product.

People want to look like they have made it, or they are doing it, but the truth is a big building will always be noticeable you can't hide it, you can only hide the small ones. What I mean is, you can't hide big brands they are that big and loud. The same applies to dreams, you cannot hide a big dream, it's too big to handle.

Most protagonists are reluctant at first but sooner than later he or she begins to respond to the call of duty. We never intended to be this big, somewhere along the way we got irritated to a point of no return. I always find it funny when people who never generated a mere 10K for a profit give us advice on profit margins. They really don't understand it, it's not in the textbook, and it comes with experience. We pushed in the corporate sector, sales, publishing, production and media and so we know what we are talking about.

Like many dreamers and doers, we often had temptations to give up but the thought of thirsty people drinking from our well kept us busy with the dream. We realized we were too deep to quit. A lot of people believed in us, some invested in us, some have designed their employment hopes around our success and we have sacrificed a lot of money, tears, energy and faith to give up now.

Give yourself time and think about all the sacrifices your Mother has done for you to go to school, the money she had to borrow and work for so that you can eat and grow. The number of times your investors believed and trusted in you even when your future in business looked dim. Think about your grandmother's efforts, how she used her grant money for your school fees and for your transport.

Pause for a minute and ask yourself, not how many times you've failed or tried but what value and experience did it all bring to you? Many people wonder why we don't quit even when the slope seem too steep. I often say to those who were bold enough to ask that we always think about quitting but remember, like suicide, life can be harder to a point where you think of it, but we don't advise you to do it. In fact, don't do it, there's always hope. Thinking about committing suicide is not a problem, but the actual act is. Don't quit your dream. Don't commit suicide.

In all the years since my matric in JKHS and time in St. Alban's College, I've learnt to manage failure and crisis. I often say I'm 10-years deep to quit. If I ever fail or fall, I prefer to do that FORWARD. I strongly believe in progress. I don't mind losing millions in the name of billions. I'm a strong believer in ALL THINGS working together for my good, when many expect me to disappear, I find new ways to COME BACK.

I was on the verge of quitting but my love for writing bailed me out. As a publisher, I've made countless mistakes and often felt like giving up. I soon realized that the invested years were WORTH IT. I was TOO DEEP TO QUIT. Every struggle in your life has shaped you into the person you are today. Maximize and monetize the experience. Never ever give up.

I felt like an outsider in a company of small dreamers.

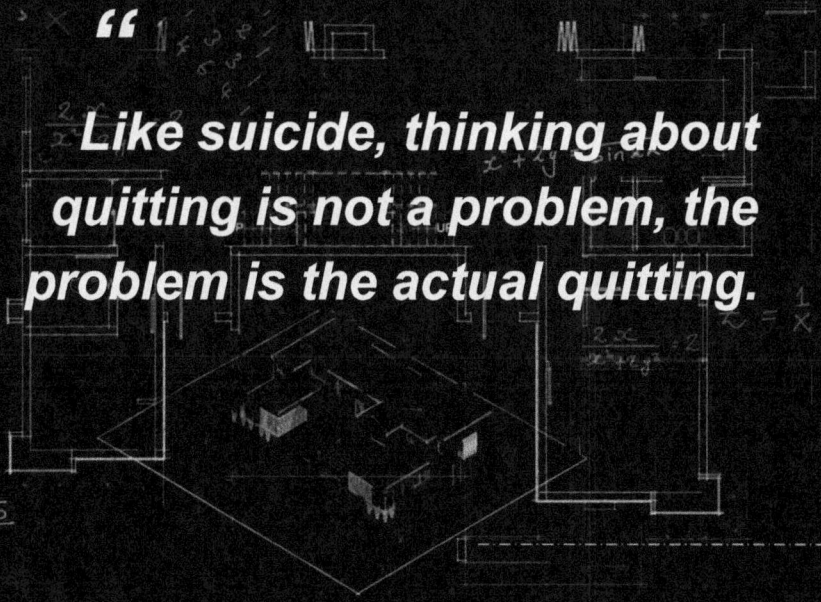

Like suicide, thinking about quitting is not a problem, the problem is the actual quitting.

5.

Meaningful Associations

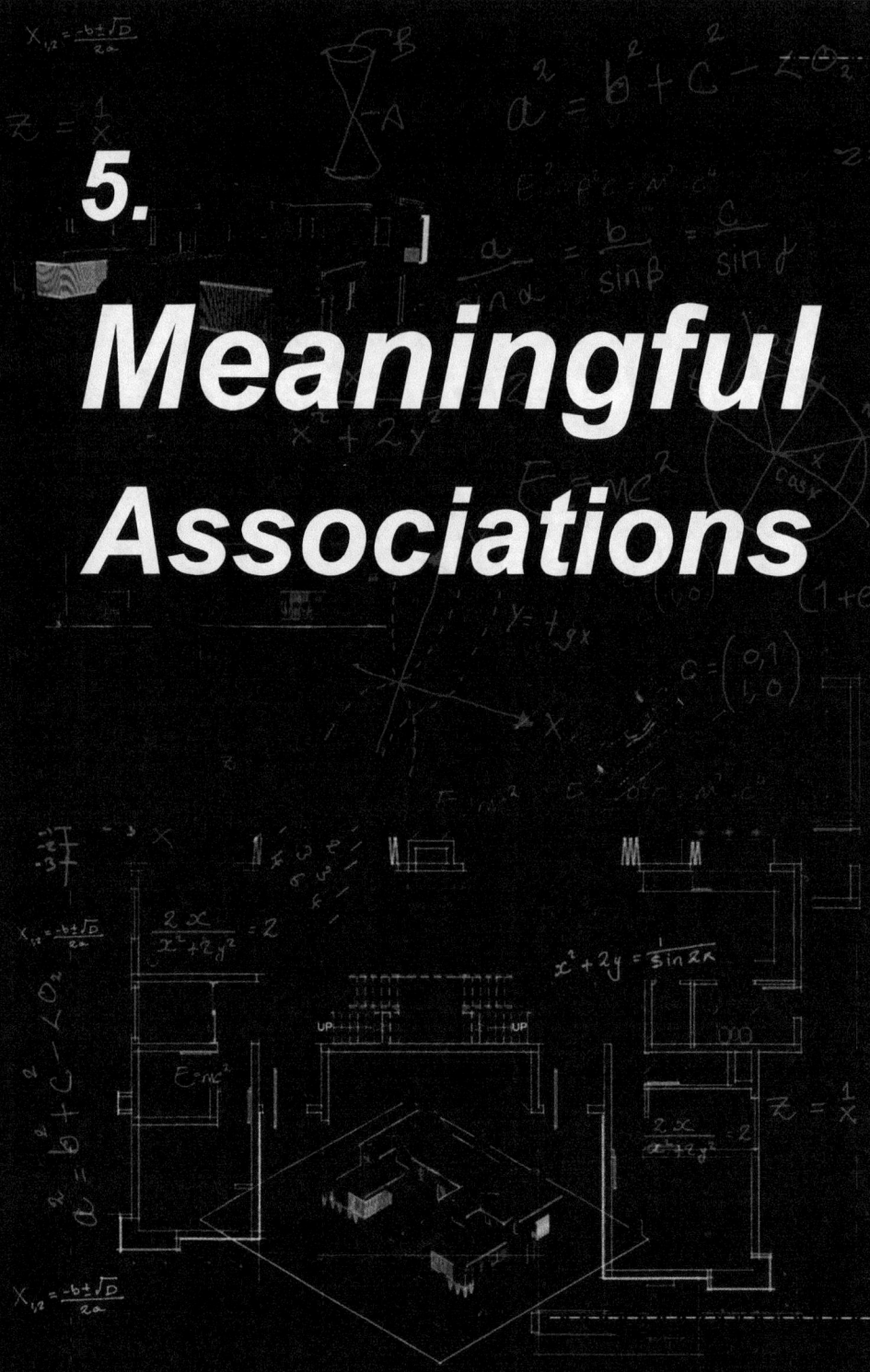

Even though I'm a pastor, worked as a professional motivational speaker, I connect to a handful of people, local and international in various fields. I connect to *Lyor Cohen*, music executive, worked at Rush Productions, Def Jam, Warner Music Group, 300 int. currently Head of YouTube music. His confidence in life & business, sense of conviction, he pays no attention to haters and naysayers.

I admire the two Indian women; *Priyanka Chopra & Indra Nooyi*, I learn from Priyanka that confidence is everything, perception is reality, she became miss world at age 18 in 2000, currently she's a well-known international actress, model, singer and philanthropist from India. Indra, is an Indian-American business executive, former chairperson and CEO of PepsiCo. 2017 was her final year at PepsiCo. To this day, everyone who know me will tell you that my favourite drink is Pepsi, it's not about the drink but the story.

In Acting, I go with the mafia guys; Joe Pesci, Al Pacino and Robert Dinero, with my all-time favourite actor, Denzel Washington. Denzel seems to be adding his soul to everything he does, he entirely commits, and I like that. He doesn't act, he owns a scene, and he takes charge of the character.

In writing I go with JM Coetzee, Bessie Head and Chinua Achebe. In pastoral and lifestyle, I connect with Bishop Clarence McClendon, gospel musician and pastor at Full

41

Harvest Church (LA), his influence is recognized by heads of states, ambassadors and celebrities who regularly call him for counsel. Bishop Clarence is not the richest pastor in the world, I'm not even writing this to debate doctrine or anything like that but to highlight my admiration. He's a man of influence and affluence, I like that.

On our second NBP seminar in association with Touch HD and Jack Daniels, I pointed out to participants largely business owners that I don't mind losing money but my VISION. I trade money for what I want. After all, money is a medium of exchange. Therefore, run after the vision, not the money.

There're two factors I want you to highlight, PASSION and SPEED. I see many passionate dreamers who operates at a very slow pace. They love what they do, they just can't act pronto. They become reactive and not proactive. They wait for us to write a book, then they follow.

I'm fully convinced that Abram Lincoln in his quote, "Things may come to those who wait, but only the things left by those who hustle", speaks to speed. As a matter of fact, amongst many, the word HUSTLE means to hurry or rush. Which leads to my question, can you really call yourself a hustler when you're that slow?

Great analytics, results from mastering categorical data, and projecting customer wants looking at the numbers. Many brands and businesses fell off by overlooking this very important element of smart advertising, proactivity, leading your customers. Don't react to what's trending on the market, project and make your bets.

> There's a huge difference between resigning and getting fired, one is reactive, and the other is proactive – Mr Kika

Game changers prospect industries by introducing trends and new technology. People who determine when to move from VHS to Digital, analogue to smart TV, pay phones to smartphones and so on. We were already preaching data value and digital content before covid-19.

The biggest question GAME CHANGERS ask as I would imagine is WHAT'S NEXT? Steve Jobs even though fired from his very own company, went on to start a company called NEXT. It wasn't long before APPLE INC. brought him back.

If only students applied for courses with this knowledge in mind, maybe we wouldn't be having an alarming rate of dropouts and unemployed graduates. People are still not asking the right questions. When you start your business, don't just team up with anyone or everyone, ask yourself the right questions, what expertise am I missing? What's his or her part in this association? Is he or she that important for this association to a point of contract?

We became co-writers after having asked fundamental questions, one has the touch, and one has craft. We both love to inspire and make an impact. What is Mr. Kika bringing on the table? And what is Mr. Banks bringing on that very table?

Successful innovations are often preceded by meaningful associations. For instance, Mark Zuckerberg had Dustin Moskowitz, Eduardo Saverin in starting Facebook back in in 2004, Steve Jobs had Steve Wozniak in the early days of Apple Inc. Bill Gates had Paul Allen, Richard Branson had Nik Powell, Sean Carter 'Jay Z', had Damon 'Dame' Dash and Kareem 'Biggs' Burke in creating Rocafella Records, Russell Simmons partnered with Rick Rubin in building Def Jam Recordings, 1984.

South Africa is not different to this phenomenon, Kalawa was founded by a jazz legend, Don Laka, Dj Oskido and Dj Christos. Kalawa Jazmee Records developed with many other directors. The story of MoFaya, the energy drink follows a similar fate of meaningful associations, Siphiwe Likhuleni Shongwe, a chemical engineer by profession understood the value and the business sense of teaming up with Dj Sbu on this energy drink business endeavour.

Like parasitic relationships, some associations are just toxic and worthless. You cannot afford to be in a draining and derailing relationship. You deserve to mutually benefit and be improved by that association. When you give in, it's only fair that you also get out. There must be transparency on the table of association. Your input and gain must not be questionable.

Often in business many think of money as the only source of contribution, overlooking time, energy, and intelligence the other partner may be contributing. Money is not the only resource in measuring meaningful associations. Sometimes the one with money has no brains.

Happiness is a commodity much more valuable than gold. Men can amass all the gold he can but if he be unhappy, that gold loses value for his life. It's no secret why we have so many miserable billionaires and millionaires in the world today. The Holy book writes that the love of money is the root of all evil. We believe that your view of money may as well be the reason of your riches or poverty.

Sometime during my varsity years, I had an opportunity to develop Wanja Chabaari's YouTube videos, on her series of Points to Live By as a 20 something year old, she began by saying HAPPINESS IS AN INSIDE JOB. Her message suggests that true happiness is found within. Many of us rely on other people for our very own peace and joy and that shouldn't be the case with you. Today, Wanja is a happily married successful Mathematician.

Today, it's necessary that we remain true to our values and ethics as we hustle. As a young Preacher back in the days, I had opportunities to make it in life only if I'd complied with terms from certain members and families, I refused and suffered the consequences of integrity. Always ensure that you associate with the right partner and energy, don't ever sell-out on your principles and dream.

Raymond Ackerman often teaches students or any businessperson who'd listen about the FOUR LEGS OF A RETAIL TABLE principle, he says the CONSUMER, and not the shareholder sits on top of the table. Mr. Ackerman emphasizes that as retailers you're there to maximize your consumer and not to maximize profit.

I chose Mr. Ackerman's' retail principles to convey my message of integrity and meaningful associations. It's very important for us to stand for something so that we don't fall for anything. We need to identify our values and principles so that we don't fall prey to power mongers.

Choose your friends wisely, SET GOALS and make it your life mission to achieve those goals. The magic concoction is characterized by meaningful associations. Who's in your mix? Who's in your circle? What's in your menu of life? Some people must be deleted from your contacts entirely, no apologies.

Have a DREAM, have GOALS, and most importantly, have a VISION for your life. A dream can be defined as your life desires in an image form, Goals may as well be defined as practical steps to achieving that image. And a vision, however, can be defined as your view or perspective of that dream. When the groundwork is ready and set, find yourself a great team.

Protect your dream and mind your surroundings. The common street word says you're the average of the five people you hang around with. The Holy Book attests in the first book of Corinth, the fifteenth chapter and the thirty third verse that 'do not be misled bad company corrupts good character'. Mr. Miller (high school teacher) often dismissed the assembly with the following words, 'show me your friends, and I'll show you your FUTURE'.

"

It's not about the failure but what we learn from the series of failure.

"

Don't ever trade your happiness for money ... that's important.

"

There's a huge difference between resigning and getting fired, one is reactive and the other is proactive.

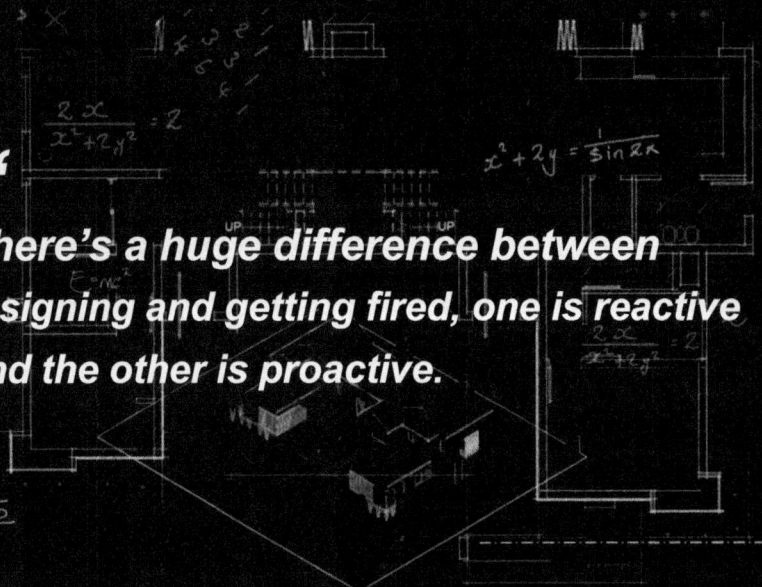

6.
Hustlers College

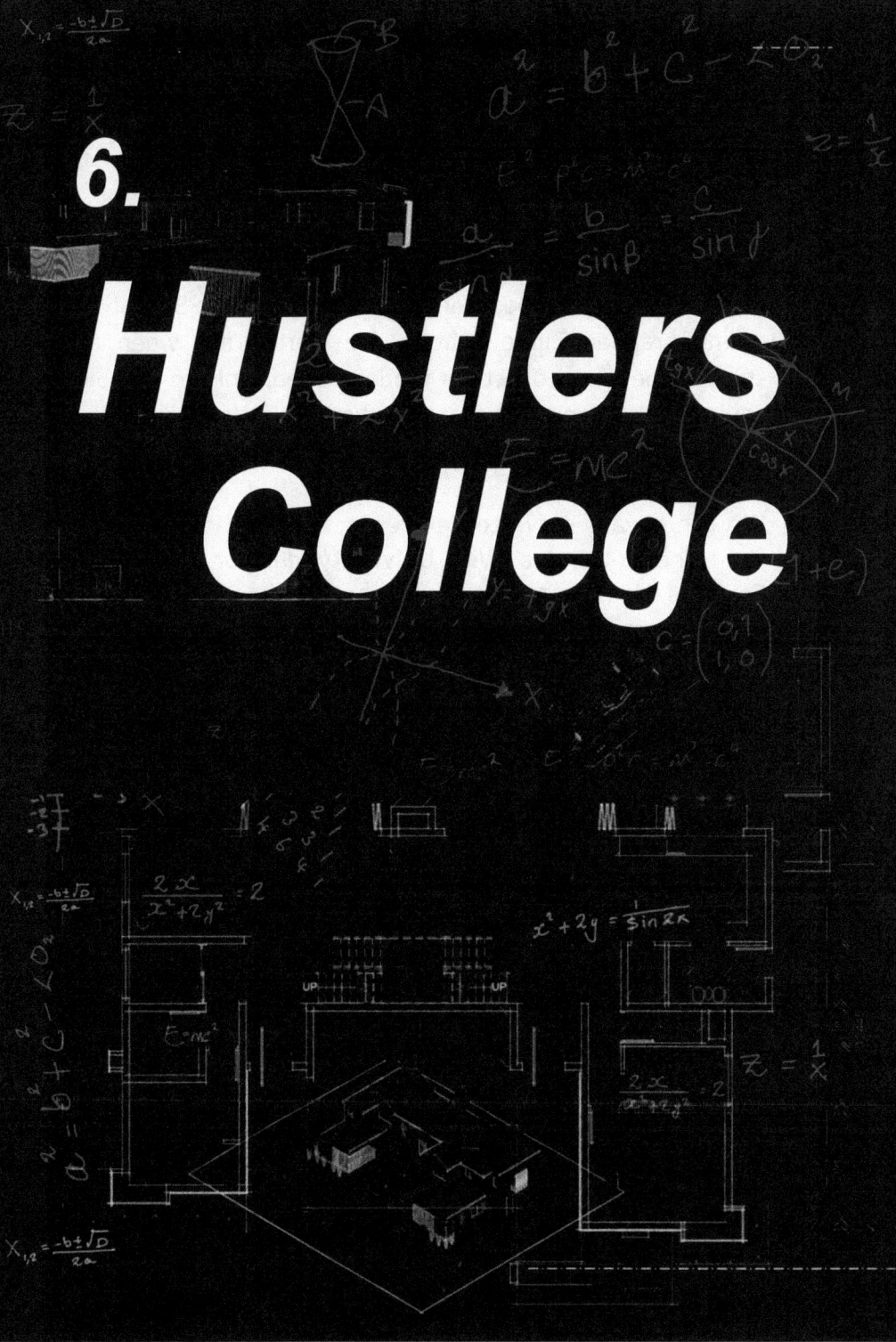

"I ordered a part and watched a YouTube on how to fix it"
- Alex Fourie

iFix founder, Alex Fourie has always been into starting his own businesses. So far, he started 50 'projects' as he likes to call them. From organizing international tours for top SA bands to selling branded Zippo lighters. He started iFix when as a student, he tried to get his iPod repaired, only to be told it could not be done and that he'd have to get a new one. He refused to buy that and decided to fix it himself.

We can always strive to be greater. Collin Thornton started from the bottom, a Wits University *dropout* in Computer Sciences. He had no money when he had the vision of starting his own company of fixing computers. He organized about *R5000* from friends and family and began marketing his soon to be the big business, (Dial-a-Nerd).

I was a Top student in High School, I graduated from the University of Pretoria (UP). I am also from the streets, informal settlements and from a Corporate World. My last job I reported to a CEO at AutoZone as a business Analyst.

I am aware of the difference in quadrants. Formal education is great, amazing, teaches you a lot but we can't deny the fact that what you learn in formal education does not connect with the reality of our modern environments. You learn nothing about Johannesburg CBD, Pretoria, Hillbrow and coins companies pay you as an intern and expect you to survive. You learn nothing about financial literacy, intuition and resilience.

Informal education is so critical that if you understand it well you can maneuver everywhere. If you are a geek from a programming class and don't like talking to people, you will find it difficult to navigate and build relationships in a world where it's more about who you know. If you find a job but still don't like congested places, you'll have difficulty maneuvering the streets of Jozi or Pretoria. It's hard getting a taxi opposite Bloed Street mall or at MTN taxi rank if you can't communicate and work your way around meandering streets.

Formal education has people spending years looking for a job to do things they already know how to do. They wait for someone to come and tell them what to do to become active. Informal education teaches you to find a way where there isn't much, that's why a lot of successful leaders were raised by parents from informational education. They utilized and monetized the little resources and skills for a greater course.

They taught these Champions how to navigate, how to study without food in their stomachs and how to persevere and remain hopeful where there's no light. Formal education teaches you more logic, which is great and helpful but there's a thin line that connects everything and that's faith and intuition. Your intuition or vibrations can help you make wise decisions. Such vibrations build a lot of major corporations but as the company grows, they depend more on what worked before, they want you to be reactive than proactive, you cannot lead by following.

Formal education is for people who follow what has already been done mainly even if they argue this, but they know 90% of people do the same thing every day because they operate like machines. They clock in, write a report, make calls, attend meetings, and go to lunch and print documents.

Machines will only replace formally educated people, people who are taught to operate like a program, the industry will continue to benefit the few percent if formally educated people operate like programs. It's easy to predict their steps and their next move. I can tell you when they will buy their next car or house or when will they get married just looking at how they live. They want certainty, formal education teaches you facts and logic, informal education teaches work and gut feeling.

'When compared to his friends, Arkad is less educated, What's stopping them from being even more successful?'

As indicated the story of Babylon shares sentiments with South Africa. Both places are rich in natural resources and a small group value more than the large group. In both places the 90/10 rule applies, 90% of the population contributes about 10% in the economy and the 10% group contributes 90% in the economic development.

Statistically speaking you will find an elite group, about 5% - 10%, carrying the rest of the population economically. The reality is 7 if not 8 out of 10 new businesses in SA fail within the first two years, for a variety of reasons, lack of relevant skills, funds and vision. Where there's no vision, people perish.

To elaborate on my point, I'll refer from the book: 'You Can't Fly To Heaven in A Straight Line' by Marvin Philips, in chapter 3:

A story about Slatersville Junior College that decided to upgrade its image. They decided that every member of the faculty and administration should have a doctor's degree. Well, they found one Janitor that not only didn't have a degree but was illiterate as well. So, they quickly fired him. But he was a positive thinker. He took the savings he had and bought an old dump truck and began hauling for a living. He did well at it. And before long, he had to buy a second truck, and then a third.

Then he bought a new one, and another, and another. He finally approached his banker saying, "Bob, I've got to have a million-dollar loan to expand business." The banker said:

"Tom, it's a pleasure to do business with you. Your trucking business is a credit to this community. You employ a lot of people and do great business. My board has instructed me to loan you the million dollars. I've already prepared the papers. All you have to do is sign the loan and the million dollars is yours."

Well, Tom said, "Bob, I hate to tell you this, I really do. But I can't read and write. You're going to witness my cross -X on that loan", and this just blew the bankers mind.

"You mean you've done all this without being able to read and write? Where would you be if you'd just had an education?" and Tom replied, "I'd be a Janitor at Slatersville Junior College". How can an illiterate person like Tom turn into a millionaire just like that?

In my knowledge asking how Tom did it is naïve. It assumes you don't recognize his education and judging by the ending of his story, he has important qualities of a businessman. Qualities not taught in 'schools. Remember, Tom had a choice; he could have applied to further his studies, give up and grow poor or rather blame himself for being illiterate for the rest of his life like many do today.

"In keeping in mind that we are the most educated immigrant in America, Africans can be found in thousands in universities and colleges throughout as academics".

(Chika Onyeani, Capitalist Nigger)

We believe that our education system trains us to ignore our natural intelligence and skills thus prepares us to work for corporations. We are never introduced to ourselves neither encouraged to discover and enhance our gifts. All we are enforced and obliged to do is to adhere to the system.

Hence, we submit that education has turned most of us into zombies, government dependents and ordinary citizens. We are not taught to be employers; we are taught to be outstanding employees. The system is designed to make us obedient disciples, clearly not outstanding leaders. In school, we are taught to fear the future as opposed to embracing it.

Informal education is so critical that if you understand it well you can maneuver everywhere. On the good side of social media, a piece of information about the Japanese schooling system was found throughout platforms. According to that information, in Japanese schools, the students don't get any exams until they reach the 4th grade. Why? Because the goal for the first 2 years of school is not to judge the child's knowledge but to establish good manners and character. They value manners before knowledge. We must review our education system.

It's not what you know or understand that gets you to the top, it's what you do about it that elevates you to the top or sinks you to the bottom. Correct me if I'm wrong, some people don't do well in theory but excel in practice. You may disagree if you may but sometimes especially to some learners, mathematics doesn't make sense on paper, it starts to ring a bell when they're on board with business.

Who said you need to know integers to count your employees? You don't even need to know any chemical reaction if we can boil water and make tea that's enough chemistry for us. In Germany you only get about 20% that makes it to tertiary, the other 80% looks for opportunities such as internships, practically oriented institutions, businesses and more options to advance themselves. In Italy, the youth is working the land (agriculture) to alleviate unemployment.

Most teachers are employees.
How can they teach kids about entrepreneurship?
-Dr. Luntz

I completely agree with Martin Prew on the basis that we need a national debate on education. Now we are down an unknown road without a map – we don't know where we are going, what point we're at, how far we must go or where our destination is.

What kind of education system do we want? What is the purpose of our education system, he said? What do business and industry want out of education? What do parents want? Martin continued to say, "We are also conflating schooling with education, and that is having a negative impact on basic education".

J. B Fuqua, industrialist, philanthropist. Never attended college but learned about business by checking out books from Duke University library through the mail, and he later donated $ 36 million to support a business school at Duke.

Julie Laipply realized she was on the wrong career path during her fourth year in tertiary. I on the other hand, had to spend five years after doing other things before realizing exactly what to study for. With the Americans, it started weigh back, from the Benjamin Franklins, Abraham Lincolns, the Henry Fords, Andrew Carnegies and even before, men of little education found ways to become the most valuable individuals not only in their native country but worldwide.

> Everyone is born a genius, but the process of life de-geniuses them" - R. *Buckmister Fuller*

In 1997, the book *Rich Dad Poor Dad* was self-published because every publisher they offered it to turned it down. *The book* has become the number one personal finance book of all time. It was on the New York Times best seller list for over six years. To date, it has sold over *30* million copies worldwide, has been published in *53* languages and is available in *109* countries.

The irony is Robert Kiyosaki (author) failed English twice in high school. He failed because he could not write, could not spell and because the teacher did not agree with what he was writing.

In the policy brief of the African Institute of South Africa, briefing no. 72, March 2012, titled, 'The failing standards of basic education', by Brenda Matshidiso Modisaotsile, opens with the following line: 'In South Africa there are many signs that show there is a crisis in education'.

We need not only to ask frank and critical questions but also provide ANSWERS and SOLUTIONS to our struggles as a nation. It's about time that we begin to think beyond our very own bread and butter. A Country's economy cannot look good when only 5%, if not less is economically emancipated. The GDP per capita counts for more, it seeks contributions not from some of us but ALL of us. The calculations should not be generic but detailed and considerate to the poorest resident.

Welcome to the next level.

"

Machines will only replace formally educated people.

"

Informal education teaches work and gut feeling.

"

'When compared to his friends, Arkad is less educated,

What's stopping them from being even more successful?'

7.

Relevance

The right knowledge for you is IMPACT and PROFIT, any other knowledge is noise and it's just there to waste your time. Building brands is my sport, products are produced in the factory, but brands are produced in the mind. Take a masterclass from those who came and did it before you.

Find materials such as mentors and books to support and empower your vision. We believe that there's many people who pray and wish to see you succeed. People who are to carry you through, those cheering you on in the balconies to push through the end. We are talking about those who succeeded in what you are doing and those who helped you identify your talent, and those who believe in you and cheer you on. Don't listen to naysayers, those who say you're good for nothing except poverty and death. You're valuable, you're a creator, and you can do amazing things.

PW Botha, last Prime Minister and the first executive President of South Africa said it bluntly when he wrote in one of his letters that the natives are good for nothing but sex. Or better yet in the book, GOLD, DIAMONDS & WAR by Martin Meredith under the chapter, The Sphinx Problem, Smuts and Merriman from the Cape had a heated discussion in a convention and Merriman argued for a limited, uniform franchise, like the Cape's system, for reasons of expediency:

"I do not like the natives at all and
I wish we had no black man in South Africa".

This is not a book on race politics but human willpower and mindset. History has proven to us that slavery mind-set can become a life-long process even after redemption. No wonder some of our people are still suffering from a long-gone system of Apartheid. Some of our people fail to reach their potential because of this mental programming. They fear what they do not know.

When the Israelites were freed from Egypt, they continued with a slavery mentality to serve in all accounts. They urged Aaron into arranging a god they can worship since Moses was wasting time. Some people would have used the opportunity to dine and chat while waiting for Moses, but they desperately needed something to worship.

'It's futile to be thinking about what happened in the past. We are thinking about what is happening now and what should happen tomorrow'.

NELSON MANDELA (FORMER PRESIDENT OF THE
DEMOCRATIC REPUBLIC OF SOUTH AFRICA)

Bansir and Kobbi are two best friends who met to discuss their misfortune from the book, Richest Man in Babylon by George Clason. In the book, we learn that they studied under the same master and in neither games nor studies did Arkad (High school friend) outshine them. Thus, they spend hours questioning his success. They don't believe an ordinary citizen, the man known to have been an average student can be the richest man in Babylon so sudden.

I call them, 'The Knowers', people who know a lot. A typical household should have at best one. That uncle who knows a lot. The one you go to when you need help with your homework or need information about what course to study, car to buy or simply find directions to a certain place. We even give those nicknames, The Encyclopaedia, Google and so forth. If you were to visit their school years, you will realize they were amongst the top students if not the only. Teachers will confirm their intelligence and classmates will agree to their academic excellence. By the look of their school performance, you would guarantee their future success before its occurrence. After ten years since my matric, I can confirm that the brightest in class are not necessarily the brightest in the future, rules are different this side.

> Master, I knew you to be a hard man,
> reaping where you have not sown and
> gathering where you have not scattered
> seed.'

It came to pass when a master called his employees and distributed talents to them per their abilities. He gave to the first, 5 talents, 2 talents to the next and 1 talent to the last and immediately went on his journey. On his return, he received both good news and bad. The first two employees multiplied their talents by two and the last employee had this to say, "I was afraid, and went and hid your talent in the earth. See, here you have what is yours?"

You will find the rest of the story in Matthew 25, what you need to know now is that the master wasn't happy with him at all. To the first two employees, more opportunities and responsibilities were given and to the last, even what he had was taken and given to the one who had more.

One would say, the last employee knew a lot, he should have used his knowledge to his advantage. Well, that's exactly my point. The last employee is no different to Deon (he thinks he's better than all his friends and yet still has nothing), Bansir and Kobbi. He would argue that the other employees benefited from his labor the same way Bansir and Kobbi would argue that Arkad's riches is all the result of Algamish.

Knowers are good justifiers and shifters of blame. They refuse to take responsibilities. When things go wrong, it's probably someone else to blame. The government is corrupt, teachers didn't explain, God is unfair, the system is rigged, or they simply cook-up a story to cover themselves.

In modern day, they justify their poverty saying the following, she comes from a wealthy family, your methods are unethical, school is not for everyone, they say. They simply talk too much and have nothing to show to back their talk. Some people still believe in the universal road, that's fine if they expect the same results as those who used the road before. The ball is now in your court, you decide which road to take. There's no one to stop you but yourself. Whether you use your money for business, self-education or formal education depends on what you want to achieve after everybody has finished speaking. Whatever you decide, prepare to stick to it.

When you're close to being great, you feel it inside; you feel the excitement and fear simultaneously. You feel the vibrations of the potential energy in your muscles and brain cells. Eventually your body and mind become the battlefield of anxiety, uncertainty and doubt. It is by this time that you must be ignorant to the negatives and focus on the positives. As you keep on pursuing the same plan that will make you great, the feeling that occurs as the feeling of reality will constantly visit you. You will occasionally feel it's impossible to make it per your target plan.

Products are produced in factories, but brands are produced in the mind. We believe that great things come to great people. You must be great to make great decisions. Jimmy Johnson's question has been one of the key questions that made me decide on what I really wanted, a safe life or a great life. And that I believe is your question as well, BUILD YOUR BRAND.

We agree, people are not just eating and sleeping. They try to do something with their lives, they apply to go to college, email their CV's, they register their initiatives and join church organizations to prove their zeal to succeed. We feel and commend on that. However, when they inevitably fail at first, they lose the initial vigor to continue and thus drop-out or quit, "But I've tried it three times already!" "I cannot do this anymore!" they quit not knowing how close they were to the golden crown.

When you use the route, everybody has been using also expect similar results as those who used the route before. For instance, if you follow the crime route, what do you expect? Do you expect a master's degree, a cheeseburger with fish and chips? Remember, as Dr. Francois Human often told us in Film School, LIFE IS A TEST OF DECISION MAKING.

Jimmy Johnson's Question:

'Do you want to be safe and good, or
Do you want to take chances and be great?'

Jimmy Johnson, the coach who led the Dallas Cowboys football team to two consecutive Super Bowl championships in 1991 and 1992. The above question calls for crucial times and I believe as a people, we come across incidences and instances where we really must ask ourselves this question not only for clarity but direction.

The battle is in the mind, mental programming, our people suffer from reliance. It's difficult almost impossible for them to survive alone. In everything they do, they need help. When they record songs, they need record labels. When they do business, they need partners and when they write books, they automatically assume that they will need publishers. Even when they have the necessary resources to get a book published, they still believe they need publishers.

From the book, 7 MEN, And the Secret of Their Greatness, by Eric Metaxas indicates to us how the resident of Mount Vernon, George Washington won his battles, power temptations and became great in the process by default. You too have the potential to be great. AMERICA is today what Mr. Washington was then, strategic and only fiddling in valuable wars and affairs for later gain.

It is the WASHINGTON'S-EFFECT that affords the AMERICANS the wisdom to capitalize in distant WARS for gain, it is that very effect that credits the AMERICANS access to raw materials from Countries such as South Africa and re-sell the products to that very Country. We know that iPhone comes from AMERICA and founded by Steve Jobs, but it's never emphasized that iPhone is manufactured in CHINA.

When other country's fear for their economy and lives, THE AMERICANS assumes CONTROL. The WASHINGTON'S EFFECT has allowed the Americans to sell its brand through media at large (TV, print, and films). Their films hypnotized the rest world into product placement and an image of America as nothing but a safe- haven, AN AMERICAN DREAM. This they do because the AMERICANS BELIEVE, at times in the inconceivable. The former President JF. Kennedy once enlarged the AMERICAN horizons by publicly declaring, "WE ARE GOING TO THE MOON".

Elon Musk, born in Pretoria, South Africa pointed out in an interview that he had to go to the United States of America to make his dreams possible. Today, he's the founder of SPACEX, said to be an American company and initiative. He too believes in going to the moon, a city called Mars.

When Mandla Maseko died late in 2019, I was very disappointed at how the media ran his story. The headlines from some online sites and papers wrote, THE SPACEBOY DIES. Mandla and I grew up in the same street in Soshanguve block G, he meant a lot to us. He represented POSSIBILITIES to many Soshanguvens and South Africans. I strongly believe we can do better in telling his story and many stories like his.

I'm a born deal maker and a deal maker. I couldn't work in a company that cuts us unless I'm the one cutting. It's very difficult to employ an unemployable individual like myself. I grew up watching my mother making means for us to eat. At age 7, my mother and I sold mangoes at the entrance of Soshanguve, block L. Nobody knew that very morning we had iced milk for breakfast.

Three months after being rejected by mainstream publishers, I self-published my first copy. I raised over 25K from sales and two laptops, one from my mother and another from someone else. From pen and paper to two laptops and 25K that's the moral of the story. Unfortunately, we are living in a society that celebrates mediocrity and devalues motivation. We have agreed to become consumers and not producers. And to the few that hustle to produce, we close oxygen by gatekeeping and bombarding them with legalities and logistics to block entry.

We don't dream, we rely on dreamers to provide us with initiatives. We are forever forced to understand and believe that South Africa is just a child who is still finding his feet in democracy. Till when, nobody knows. When I was doing my matric in 2009, the pass mark was 40%, now the pass mark is 30%. If the sequence is consistent then in 20 years, the pass mark will probably be 10% if not 0%.

No one sees danger if the Department of Education and Principals celebrate their 100% pass rate. The instant gratification disease has left us broke and in dire debt. Our incoming leaders are not only inheriting positions from the outgoing leaders, but they also inherit oversights and systematic burdens.

If you're going to talk about the things you don't do, you'll always be following those who start. Apparently, it's okay for the government to lower the matric pass rate, increase university intake by providing loan schemes to 'disadvantaged children'. From an early age we were taught to clap when someone gives or hands us something. Why change the norm now? The youth just want to graduate. They want to become managers and CEOs.

If you care to ask an unemployed graduate why he/she's still unemployed, the response will directly point to the government. In South Africa the government must pay when one is born, pay for one to go to school, find one a job and probably bury him/her when he/she dies. We're living in the pointing generation.

The government-should-supply mindset has killed many dreams and goals. The core of human initiative has long been killed. Today, it's easier to join than to initiate. It's easier to follow than to lead. We talk more and act less, If not none. People like to lead, yet they don't have leadership qualities. In chaos and fire, they're the ones to run away and come back later when fire is out, and the situation is calm. We've been in the storm, we even learned to dance there.

Everybody wants to be successful in one way or another. I wanted to succeed so badly that at times, I prayed and cried. My normal day at age 10 to 16 was cutting out super cars, beautiful mansions and famous people from magazines; reading inspirational books, trying to watch Top Billing in a small black and white TV that gained its power from a small car battery. I would visualize myself already successful; I spent most of my youth days in clouds. I understand hunger, the pain of poverty and the effect of a negative environment in one's life.

I saw and learned a lot of things at an early age. Coming to think of it, I'm just like my Mother. I grew up watching her make plans for us. I was always ready and to sell mangoes to Motorists who drove by the Soshanguve entrance from Soutpan road and R80 highway with my Mother, Eva. I was motivated by her ability to make something out of what seemed to be nothing, we hoped and prayed for better days.

"

Products are produced in the factory, but brands are produced in the mind.

"

They fear what they do not know.

"

LIFE IS A TEST OF DECISION MAKING.

"

The battle is in the mental programming, our people suffer from reliance.

8.

Millionaires Factory

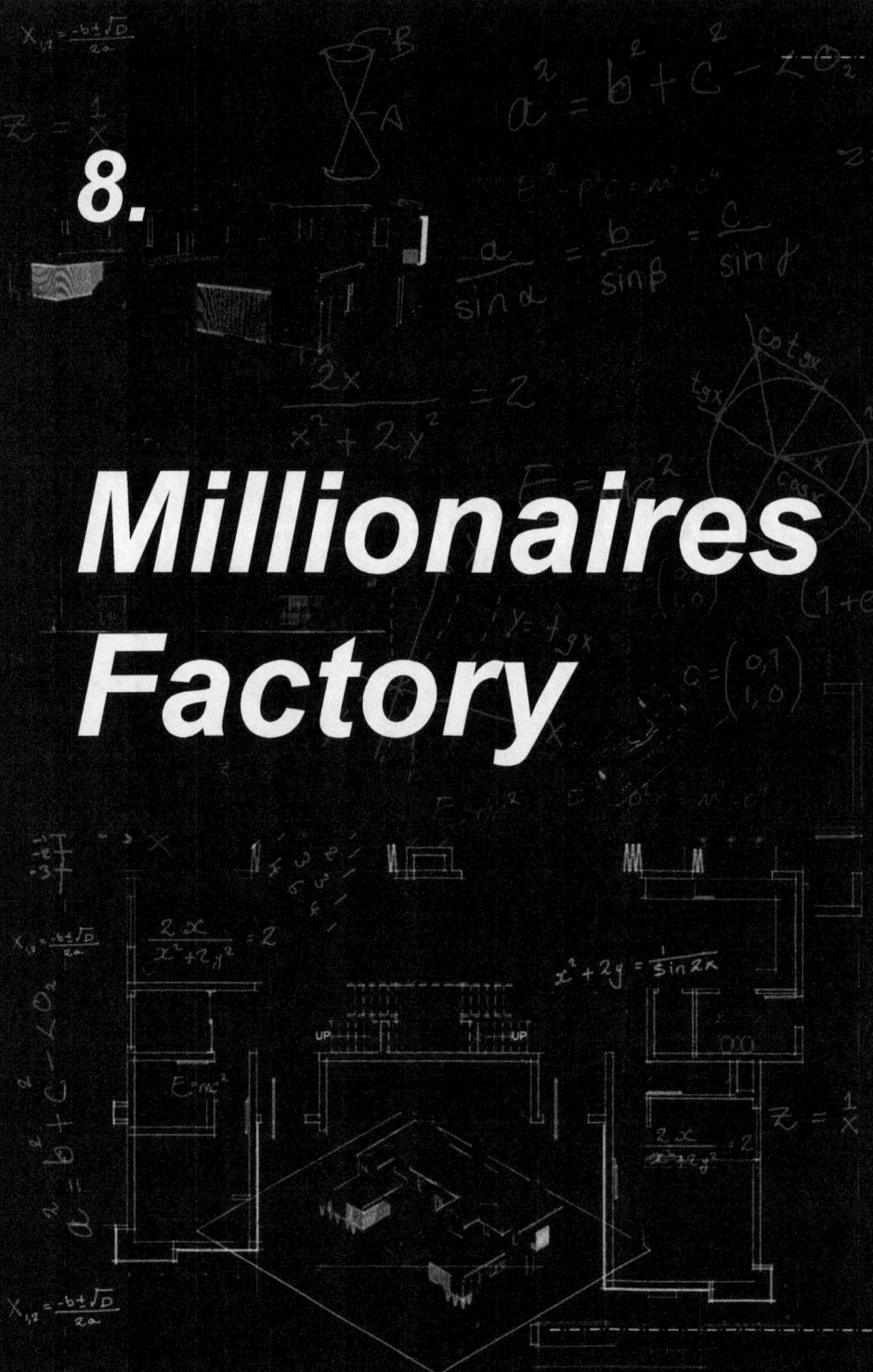

We are not moved by the assertion that Sandile Shezi, became SA's youngest millionaire at age 23, but we are moved by what he has done behind the scenes, he sacrificed his university money for his dream. He made investments and later established his Global Forex trading business. When asked for comment in a news interview he said, 'decide what you want and stick to it'. We don't trade but connect to what he did and spoke.

Cassper Nyovest, SA Rapper and businessman is without doubt a self-made millionaire. He's the son of teachers who left school at age 16 to pursue his passion for music. We have many 'pack your bags and go to Joburg' success stories in South Africa. In fact, even though it's highly risky especially today, this has turned out to be a method of success to many.

At the age of 27, Lebo Gunguluza made it to the millionaire club as a media mogul. Growing up during apartheid, losing his father in the process of changing his life, went to university with a handful of coins in his pocket, about R60 or less and a larger-than life attitude. After a little bit of networking and battering, he turned himself into one of South Africa's most charismatic, self-made millionaires.

Many years back Gayton Mackenzie was released from prison with R12 in his pocket. He had to choose either to use the money for taxi or walk. Criticized for uttering what is called 'broken'

73

English, the man rose to become a multi-millionaire, an author and one of the top motivational speakers in South Africa. The road to success is not always straight.

Raymond Ackerman was fired from his job in 1966, he persuaded a group of friends to loan him the money to buy three small 'Pick n Pay' stores, which at the time employed a total of 175 people. He bought the stores in 1967 from Jack Goldin, a little guy from Cape Town who was impressed by Raymond's business hospitality.

On his retirement, 44 years later, he influenced the retail industry in South Africa and grew his company to 792 stores in 8 Countries, employing more than 60 000 people. These are stories to tell in building this nation. According to the law of farming, the right to reap is given to the sowers and not those who wish and dream for unknown results.

It is neither preached nor emphasized (I think it must) that Refiloe Phoolo well knows as Cassper Nyovest and Senzo Vilakazi well known as Kwesta are both high school dropouts who left school at age 16 to pursue their music career dreams. Yet we are very haste in coveting their success when they fill-up stadiums, sell platinum's, appear on international media platforms. SUCH STORIES MUST BE TOLD!

South Africans don't preach motivation and this in my opinion is in the list of the leading causes of demotivation and lack of enthusiasm amongst the youth. Our youth only knows one side of the story of success.

In a Country that strongly values education, it must be BREAKING NEWS when young black self-made millionaires arise – Mr Kika

For I believe such stories can inspire hope and help stop one child who grew to believe in one route to success from giving up. We all want to know at some point that we are not alone and that what we go through is not new. It soothes the heart and fuels confidence when you know your ROLE MODEL has been through what you are currently going through.

Semester two from OG Mandino's 'University of Success' opens with a quote by S.t Jerome that states, 'Begin to be now what you will be hereafter'. We tend to procrastinate, postpone what should be done today for the next day and the day after that. We can't become because we're tricked into thinking we're becoming. It goes without saying that we were not deployed here on earth to be little more than walking vegetables. Our destiny cannot be to become earthly ornaments. There's more to this than what meets the eye. We have a lot to offer.

There's greatness within us that deserves to be unleashed. Something in us is so strong that we constantly believe in the beauty and the realization of our dreams. Let's continue to cook best stories with ingredients of patience, focus and hard work. We're often reminded that we're the masters of our own fate and so we must without doubt live accordingly.

Feed your mind and continue to water your dream even when you sometimes don't see or feel the progress, it is significant that you

75

carry on. Continue to cook, sooner or later, your dream will be ready to serve. Find courage from other people's stories and work on yours. In other words, applaud others whilst WORKING ON YOUR GRIND.

We must avoid falling into the entitlement trap, feeling like we are the rightful victims of society. It is very important that we turn the page and get on with our lives. The ugly hands of poverty, the threatening pangs of hunger, and starvation are not the divine design for our lives. Joel Eze, a friend of mine from Nigeria points out in his first book, Manual of Champions that 'our streets are painted with beggars and unemployed young men and women'.

> "When you are black in this Country and
> declare war against poverty, you declare war
> against many forces".
>
> [T-bo Touch, Annual Morning Show 'S1E58]

From the early 1870's, the diamond fever and the prospect of sudden riches excited many people as they set out in ox-wagons and mule carts heading to the desolate patch of sun-baked scrubland in Griqualand where diamonds had been discovered.

In page 30 from the book, 'Gold, Diamond and War' by Martin Meredith, we learn more from Louis Cohen who wrote about Rhodes' lack of interest in girls. He further wrote, 'I do not believe if a flock of the most adorable women passed through the street, he would have gone across the road to see them.'

What preoccupied his mind? Certainly, far more important than girls, but even more than diamonds, we are told, was the idea of obtaining a professional qualification. The point we are trying to drive home here is that he sacrificed many of the things you and I would see pleasant for his bigger goal. We are not discussing education mishaps and race politics here, but we focus on the strategy that worked and human values. Perhaps the other factor to add in your dream plan is sacrifice. What is it you want and what are you willing to sacrifice for it? 'Sacrifice' is a word poor people rather hate because it reminds them of what they continuously fail to do such as leaving their comfort zone and taking responsibility.

It is much easier for the poor to cook up stories of the illuminati and snakes in justifying their laziness and complacency – Mr Kika

There's a big difference between compromise and sacrifice, and my point is on the latter. Cecil Rhodes, according to the book mentioned, appears to have been a man of determination, commitment and set of values. BE DETERMINED and set your ETHICS and GOALS.

Zakes 'Zanemvula' Mda is without doubt in the list of South African legendary and prolific writers making waves in the international diaspora. The only way to master your craft is to keep working on it. You'll of course fail and make mistakes but most importantly you'll get better. In an interview with Thabo "T-bose" Mokwele on Kaya FM, Mr. Mda responded when asked about his writing, "The more I wrote, the more I got better".

The first print of my first book, back in 2013, about a hundred copies had grammar and technical faults. My enemies had a feast that year. Firstly, I had to own up to my oversight, cut down the selling price by 30% and communicate the error with customers for clearance. The thought of quitting never crossed my mind if it did, I wasn't paying attention. I was too busy convincing myself that my dream is possible.

I bet you a 100K that many young South Africans want to be like Zakes, Prof. Wole Soyinka, Gordimer or Bessie Head. The challenge is that they (the zealous youth) don't want to put up with the pain and the process it takes to get to that point. Perhaps, they just like the idea of it. Success is intentional and personal. Nobody succeeds by accident. As a writer, I've felt the pain of isolation and frustration when writing what appears to be a masterpiece.

Given her psychological state of clinical depression and frustration, in a train to Manchester, JK Rowling wrote better pieces of Harry Potter on a napkin. The book was heavily rejected by mainstream Publishers before its epic success that led into it being translated into various languages and adopted into a film series.

It takes time to emerge. I've heard and read about the Chinese Bamboo tree. Planted after the ground is prepared, for the first four years, all the growth is underground. The tree demands to be watered and fertilized every day without visible progress. In the fifth year, the tree grows 80-90 feet tall (about 30m) in the first five-six weeks. Anything worth waiting for must be very special. Patience is indeed a virtue.

When given an hour to cut down a tree, spend 45 minutes sharpening the axe and the remaining 15 minutes doing the actual job. It's very important to plan. Our inability to plan and strategize must come to stop if indeed our dream is that important.

> 'Success requires no explanations and failure permits no alibis.
> -Napoleon Hill (1883-1970)

I totally agree with T-bo Touch, we fight so many forces on our way up as black South Africans. Be that as it may, life will refuse us the liberty of using the very 'forces' as an excuse for our failure and inability to succeed. You become what you are, not what you want. It's very important that we begin at once to safeguard what goes in our minds. We must at all costs protect our minds in waging war against such forces.

Life is set to flow in the direction of our thoughts and affirmations. Stand guard the door of your mind and mind your language. It is in the tongue where we find the power of both life and death. It is often said that the tongue can burn the whole house down. Inversely, the same tongue can build it up.

Develop and create scenarios that build and pushes you to do and become better. Divorce friends and people who set you back. Hang around those who fuel your dreams and ideas. Don't hang around losers; those who gain entertainment gossiping about others and never about their ideas. We don't just want to make money and hide. We are not influenced by money to do what we do. That's why we will constantly educate those who are like us to follow.

It was in 2009, when my Life Sciences teacher introduced us to three types of minds; small minds discuss people, average minds discuss events and big minds discuss ideas. I'm in the latter group and it is my wish that you join in. No entrance fee just a will to change your life by executing your ideas.

Age is not an issue of concern here but the WILL TO CHANGE and SUCCEED. Samuel. L. Jackson achieved global recognition for his acting work beyond the age of 40 and Morgan Freeman at age 50. You're never late to SUCCEED. Like the Chinese Bamboo Tree, the obscured years are equally important if not more to the entire growth.

Napoleon Hill, self-help author (1883 – 1970) was born in a one-room cabin. His mother died when he was 9 years old. At the age of 15 he married a girl who had accused him of fathering her child. The girl recanted the claim, and the marriage was annulled.

Earl Nightingale since age 9, had a question he urgently needed answers to; why some people grew up to enjoy prosperity while others struggled merely to survive? He grew up in economically depressed times and that exasperated his poverty.

To address his childhood question and concerns, at age 35 he released his tape titled 'The Strangest Secret' which without anticipation sold millions of copies with the help of Columbia

Records. These are ordinary men like many who grew to change their circumstances and as a result become extraordinary. Nothing is impossible to a man or a woman who believes in self and executes his or her vision accordingly. Millionaires come from hard work, self-belief and consistency.

Remember the Chinese Bamboo Tree.

"

In a Country that strongly values education, it must be BREAKING NEWS when young black self-made millionaires arise.

"

It is much easier for the poor to cook up stories of the illuminati and snakes

in justifying their laziness and complacency.

"

You'll of course fail and make mistakes but most importantly you'll get better.

"

Millionaires come from hard work, self-belief and consistency.

9.
The Come-back Effect

Setbacks in life and in business raise questions about how far you can go as an individual. I went through all kinds of setbacks from owing office rentals and having doors closed on me, to petrol finishing on the highway and daughter getting sick while we didn't have medical aid. At times my wife got tired of me running this business, my mother has been upset with me for leaving a good paying job and my father has doubted me and thought of me as stupid.

I went through it all, I've been called all kinds of names by friends and been alienated by people who think I'll ask them for money. There have been times when I couldn't get clients because of my situation. I ran out of cash flow and doubted my business model.

This book was primarily written to address this issue, COMING BACK FROM A FALL. Today where is so easy to just throw in the towel and quit, we question our will and desire to succeed. It takes a winner to get up and keep going.

Today, everybody wants to see the proverbial ceiling first, the prize, reward or get some sense of conviction before acting. Very few works in commission-based industries because the idea of stable income is more convincing to their ears than building their own business.

The casual day dreamers cannot afford to partake in the actual process of hustling, yet they love the idea of achieving something. UTOPIA is everyone's dream. Ideally, we all want to inherit undefined riches and accumulate wealth without lifting a finger.

By default, WEALTHY people are allergic to lazy people. You'll never find a rich man in lazy town. Really successful people are hard workers. They know first-hand that for things to work, they must work. Unfortunately, we're living in an era where people want change but they're not willing to change.

> "For things to change, you've got to change. For things
> to get better, you've got to get better. " - Jim Rohn

I have lost a lot of money in starting my business, I've witnessed my associates and friends blow hundreds of thousands both in the name of FUN and HUSTLING. In this journey some losses are justified, and some are not. Even to the unjustified loses, we believe in RESILIENCE. We have the come-back effect – the ability to come back from setbacks.

It takes much more power from you to RISE UP after a ninth fall. However, we believe that when you fall nine times, get up tenth. Stay hopeful and learn to see good in people. I struggled with pessimism and negativity for a major part of my life. My attitude chased away those who truly wanted to help me PASS THROUGH. In everything thing, I was the guy who points out the bad and ten reasons why the plan won't work. Now I know that for your life to change, you must change. Today I view failure as an OPPORTUNITY.

I know of a blind man who suffered from complaining idiosyncrasy. They dished for him a plate with two pieces of chicken he then complained that if blind people receive two pieces of chicken, then people who could see got the whole chicken. They heard his complaint and gave him a full chicken he complained and said, if blind people are getting full chickens than people who see got cows. And when they gave him a cow, he continued to complain that this shows that people who see got herds of cows. Such people are never satisfied, avoid them.

Remember in as much as I believe you should place your background back and not bring it forth, I strongly believe you need to first accept your situation or rather background then work out ways to reject and fight it. One may ask, 'but, why don't I just reject it?' The thing is, just rejecting is equivalent to denying it. And you don't want to live your life in denial.

You may not have money in paper yet but if you understand the power of your name, your contacts, image, information, intelligence and access, you could start today to make conversions and enrich yourself. I quote from Stedman Graham, "People who consider themselves victims of their circumstances will always be victims, unless they develop a greater purpose for their lives."

'A man can fail many times, but he isn't a failure until
he begins to blame somebody else.'

-John Burroughs

I once read a book by Nick Vujicic, titled: Life without Limits. FIRSTLY, Nick was born without limbs and legs but due to the power of being purpose-driven Nick graduated in a double major at Griffith University with a Bachelor of Commerce in Financial

Planning an Accounting in 2003 at the age of 21. And he's one of the leading motivational speakers in the world today.

The 16th President of the United States, Abraham Lincoln couldn't have been righter when he said: "Things may come to those who wait, but only the things left by those who HUSTLE".

I come from a poor background, and I've witnessed disturbing things at an early, but I've also learnt in the scripture where it says, 'Mere talk leads to poverty'. And my creative ways of getting out of this negative web, "escape gate", was through developing a concept of 'An intelligent fool'. An intelligent fool is someone who knows and most probably understands what needs to be done but fails to do it. When he turns inevitably turns poor, he blames others.

Somewhere in the third quarter of 2009, the government launched an opportunity for excelling students in public schools to study in private schools. This was to prepare us for the final matric exams. I was in St. Albans College, right next to Varsity College. They took other students from Mamelodi High, Jafta Mahlangu, Vukani MaWethu and so forth. This opportunity helped shape my mind, my level of confidence and esteem escalated towards the right direction.

I love writing, speaking and filming hence I turned my passions into careers, I go around the Country motivating in institutions, schools, prisons and social organizations like churches. I wrote and edited several books including the one you are reading now.

What are you most passionate about? If you answered the question, then start following that passion.

Don't wait for people to call you or hire you, start right away, write that book, sing that song, apply for that job, or start your business and employ yourself, register for that course or do the opposite, dropout, quit your job and simply follow your passion. If you want to be a writer, then do what other writers do WRITE!

"I was hearing the voice of my inner soul. It was asking me to dig the place where I had found the trashes of Dry River. I laid down on the trash of Dry River and tried to listen to something.   As I started concentration, I heard something. It was a sound of flowing Underground River". - *Mr. Thakaruji*

Mr. Thakaruji and his two men found the underground flowing river in the place of Dry River. It was the first sight of success for his dream project, 'New Wonderland'. According to Birister Sharma, author of THE ROAD TO SUCCESS, Mr. Thakaruji was almost dead when his New Wonderland dream came into fruition. He sacrificed a lot, including his career, family and friends to see his vision come into physical reality.

Before very long, 'other people' came to witness and celebrate what he has built. People will always think and talk negative about your dream until YOU make it happen. The ability to ignore the naysayers and focus solely on your dream is the best thing to do for yourself.

It took six months and four days to complete the canal from the Dry River. After waiting a long time for rain there was only flying clouds in the sky, but there was no shower of rain. He even got sick waiting for a miracle. All his workers left except two of his men. Nobody saw and understood the vision only him alone. If you don't plant a tree, many people won't have shade. Some people's dreams are tied to yours.

The first year ended in both hopes and despairs. But he had a strong belief and determination that one day there will be heavy downpour in that place. "There will be water in every well. There will be water in every pond. There will be water in our canal." He said to his people.

Slowly but surely, the morals of the people of his dream project started decreasing. They gradually lost hope and patience. They lost confidence in him, but he continued regardless. He understood that RESULTS will regain his confidence. Sometimes all we need is results and certainly not hear reasons on why you failed to succeed. Indeed, failure permits no alibis.

He had to fulfil his dream to change Dry Land into 'New Wonderland'. How could he kill his lifelong dream? It was not only his dreams, but also the mission of his life. He certainly couldn't quit. He had to accomplish his mission by responding to *the crave*. He would stop at nothing until his dream-thirst is quenched.

Mr. Thakuruki had everything in place, a supportive family, an MBA from a prestigious institution, as an Indian, a wife already arranged and almost everything one could need to enjoy life. With everything in place broke out of the norm to pursue his dream, he fell and failed but still came back even more passionate.

> "Climb if you will but remember that courage and
> strength are nought without prudence, and that
> momentary negligence may destroy the happiness of a
> lifetime. Do nothing in haste; look well to each step;
> and from the beginning, think what may be the end."
> *Edward Whymper*

It was from the Theodal pass in 1789 that the Swiss physicist and geologist, Horace **Benedict** de Saussure, who had earlier scaled Mont Blanc, contemplated climbing the Matterhorn. But he felt that: 'Its precipitous sides, which give no hold to the very snows, are such as to afford no means of accesses. As we all know, one can never be completely right in this world, an English wood engraver, Edward Whymper, was to prove him wrong. Whymper made several attempts to climb the Matterhorn from the Italian side between 1861 and 1863, but in 1865, at the age of 25, he decided to try from the Swiss side. He asked the well-known Italian guide Jean Antoine Carrel to go with him, but Carrel had already been engaged by the Italian Alpine club, also preparing for an assault on the Matterhorn. During the race to the summit, Whymper moved fast. With 18-year-old Lord Francis Douglas he enlisted the aid of Peter Taugwalder, a renowned Zermatt guide who thought that the foreshortened view of the Matterhorn ridge from the Swiss side made it look steeper than it is. Others in the party were Taugwalder's son Peter, aged 22, Michael Croz, 35, a guide from Chamonix, the Reverend Charles Hudson, 37-, and 19-year-old Robert Hadow. The descent was slow and tricky, and as the party began to negotiate, a particular difficult section, tragedy struck. Hadow slipped and fell against Croz, and the two men began to slide downwards, dragging Hudson and Douglas with them. The rope snapped and the four men disappeared over the precipice onto the Matterhorn Glacier 4000ft (1200m) below. Three of the bodies were recovered the next day, but Lord Francis Douglas was never found.

Working on your dream demands that you develop a thick skin because you will be tested and tried. Some falls are more intense, many people don't come back from such downfalls. You need to understand that I used to sell in train stations, with the money hustled there I always brought home chicken mixed portions. I still remember between 2018 and 2019, we were kicked out of office and had to work at Starbucks for some time. I was scammed over 100K and faced unimaginable challenges but still I arose. Things were so dark for me in 2018, my joy was brought by *Tshedza's* birth, my daughter, and she was and still is my light. Through her I gained strength to come back and keep pushing.

"
I ran out of cash flow and doubted my business model.

"
WEALTH is allergic to lazy.

"
The come-back effect – the ability to come back from setbacks.

"
Today I view failure as an OPPORTUNITY.

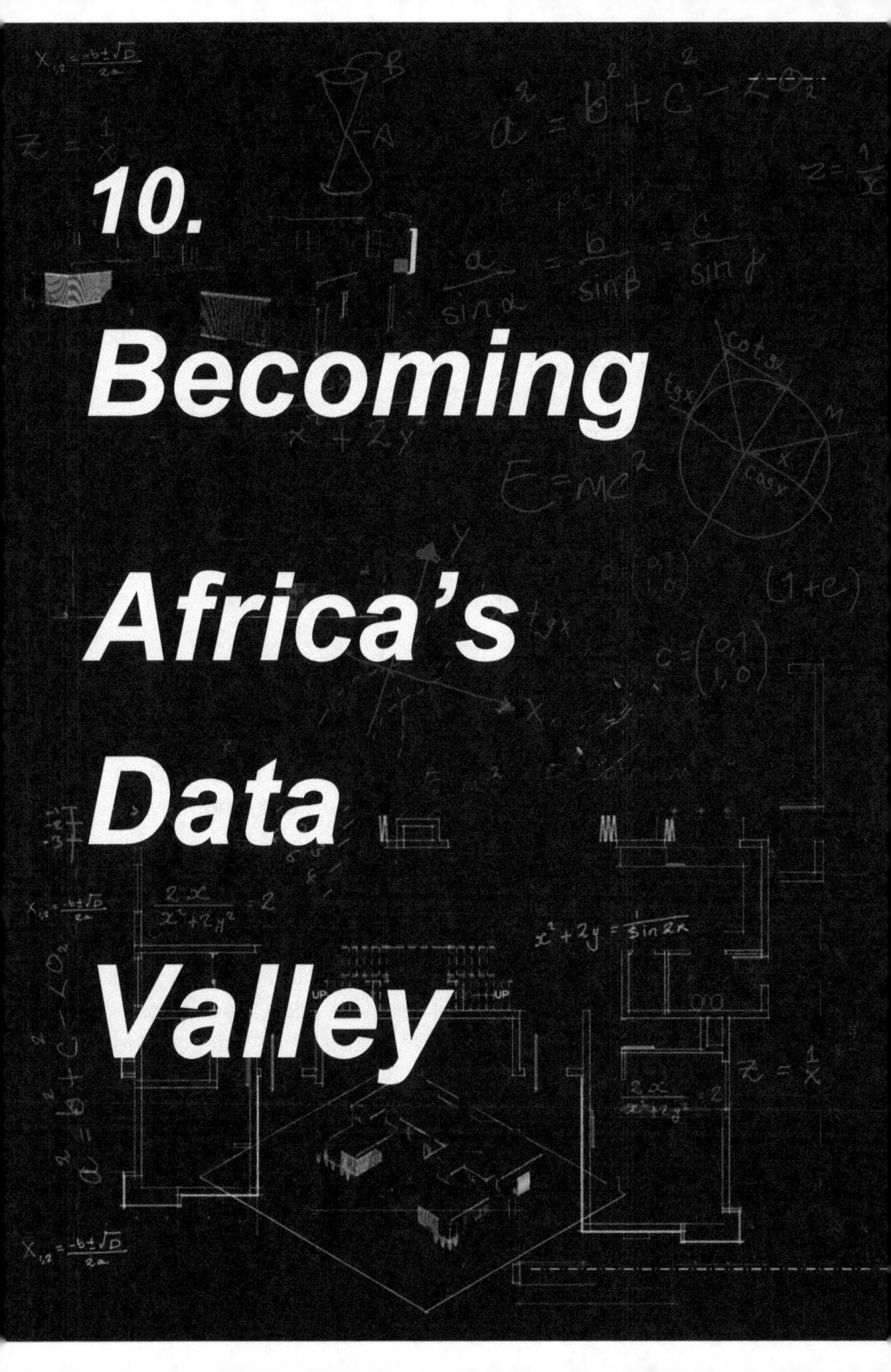

10.

Becoming

Africa's

Data

Valley

April 2020 and covid-19 just hit the world globally and everyone is shaking. We are working from home and I'm working from my garage in Centurion. Something hit me that if we are going to make a difference, let it be beyond South Africa, digital had just shown possibilities of connecting the world per second and I saw this as an opportunity to expand.

Companies started to strategize and put digital first. It was like a world shut down and everyone was trying to understand the new trend. After 2 weeks of working from home, I saw the need to restructure how we present ourselves in business. This was a self-conversation about differentiation and positioning.

We removed ourselves completely from just adding value in advertising using Data but to start using Data Engineering processes inside business and create bespoke data pipeline solutions. We started adding a team of Data Engineers and Software Engineers to start engineering what we call Africa's Data Valley today.

We became one of the fastest growing Data Technology Company in 2020 but we still learning and growing. 2021 became one of the best years of multi awards and accolades. We won 4 awards for Innovation, Technology, management of People and Department of Science and Innovation minister's award for Overall Excellence.

This was mainly because our bespoke solutions for global brands were different, agile and provided an overview understanding of Data across different departments. Companies we work with are now able to understand and integrate production, point of sale and consumer data into one central view.

2021 became a defining year and set us apart from everyone else across Africa, our communications publicly became very powerful, and people were listening to us. As a CEO, I became a Top 5 finalist on the Accenture Rising Star Awards, and this also became a game changer in the market. Our voice grew on LinkedIn and other business Professional platforms, and this is how we became the best innovative company in the continent.

Becoming Africa's Silicon Valley was stressful and amazing at the same time. As you begin to grow fast, you want to make quick and sharp adjustments to maintain that growth without fail. This is because it's easy to start making mistakes on a top-level business and you can't lose that one opportunity to change everything. It is possible to get to this level, yet it requires a different thinking too. You must be a crazy one or different kind amongst your group.

We became known as Africa's Silicon Valley when we started to tap more into who we are and that's Data Science and Tech Developments, we became a digital transformation partner for merging and large enterprises.

It's not easy to get here but we did it, while everyone was focusing on collecting money and referrals, tenders, and gift projects, I was grinding every day to build our brand, sometimes you couldn't tell where we are going or what we do.

We used all the experience from personal brands, small business and emerging business to build large enterprises for a big cheque. We became a thought leader in Data Science and spoke in different African seminars. As I'm writing, I'm a nominee for Rising Star Awards, currently Accenture Top 5 Entrepreneur 2021 Award.

We build the brand to be so powerful that it now speaks for itself and sell itself. We are in a position where our business sells itself and businesses look for us to provide solutions. We tailor make solutions according to clients' request.

We develop tech software for large enterprises, run big data analytics to give insights and strategic targeted solutions and artificial intelligence models like Robotic Process Automation to automate financial and human resource systems. To get to this level you will need a powerful brand that makes large enterprises listen to you and be attracted to you.

> "Talifhani is one of those blessed individuals with a calculus mind".

"Although I dreamt and visualized this as a goal and pursued it with confidence. I could still not believe when it happened. I was ecstatic. My model is simple but not easy, it requires a bit of intelligence, I knew this when I started".

You need to have integrity, being consistent, and bring the solution to different problems and challenges. To me, the ultimate idea is to help somebody else. In 2016, I was already recognized in the media space, I helped transform so many artists and businesses. I've accumulated the experience and knowledge needed to build this empire, I spent 2 years, between 2012 – 2014, educating my mind and developing my brain power, skills I already had.

Lesson from Dylan Du Toit's Grandfather:

My personal thought process and business acumen has been shaped by a monopoly game I played back at my friend's, Dylan Du Toit's house. In playing the game I bought the properties; I tend to always spend monopoly money on expensive buildings and stuff. Dylan's grandfather, who owned a construction business guided me and told me that this was not the right way of building and growing a business. To this day this is my business philosophy, I choose not to drive expensive cars or live in a huge mansion but rather invest it back in my business. You can't pay the salaries we pay and drive a Ferrari; you need to prioritize your vision and expansion plan.

We're now opening our second headquarters in Cape Town, V&A Waterfront. We are going to employ over hundred professionals within the next 12 months. In Analytics Advertising, we believe in growth and expansion, technology and Innovation. This year, 2022 we celebrate our 5th year anniversary in March, there's more work ahead, the market is fertile, and the future is exciting.

Applying Data technology solutions in different industries is what makes us unique. Creative advertisers and many other marketers fall in love with creating content, but they can never ask themselves who they're creating the content for. What is the customer sensitivity, Customer basket, what is their purchasing frequency and recency, their LSM and predictive modelling? Our key selling point – We create bespoke data technology solutions to help our global clients understand their customer behaviour, when to sell a product and which product to produce first at what time.

I still think the opportunity in Africa is going to be enormous especially in digital business. More and more consumers in Africa are becoming enlightened and tech ready. The trick is to increase your online presence and impact. My family keep me grounded, I have a wife, Pabalelo and two babies, Tshedza and Tyson.

I take them to school and pick them up after, this keep me on track with my husband duties. I'm the answer to what God knew will be a question in my generation. When you find what you love, pursue it and keep going. Always listen to those who've walked the road you're embarking on.

"

*Becoming Africa's Data Valley was
stressful and amazing at the same time.*

"

*We became known as Africa's Data Valley
when we started to tap more into who we
are as a company.*

"

*I was grinding every day to build our
brand, sometimes you couldn't tell
where we are going or what we do.*

"

*You can't pay the salaries we pay and
drive a Ferrari, you need to prioritize your
vision and expansion plan.*

11.
The Rise Of Salmon

> Having lived in informal settlements for more than a decade, I realized that the world doesn't come to a standstill because you're unemployed and nor does your country under-develop because you failed to develop". – Mr Kika

For years I held a deep desire to graduate from a higher learning institution. On the 4th of May in 2018, I was glad to attend a graduation ceremony for a qualification in TV & FILM Production from Tshwane University of Technology (TUT). Indeed, dreams do come true, I didn't want to be employed or anything, I just wanted to graduate.

After Mr. Banks and I met for the first time in his Rosebank office, we agreed to collaborate. We both had an ambition to grow beyond our current circumstances. We shared a strong desire to reach out and share this newly discovered phenomenon with the rest of the world. In essence, BEYOND AMBITION denotes the burning desire, fire and passion that constantly wins the debate against our temptations to give up.

The obsession to succeed has left many of our young men and women depressed and paralyzed. On the other hand, the joy it brings has left many of us excited, enthusiastic and optimistic about the future. It is the total embodiment the vision Mr. Banks and I carry for this book. Having identified that this concept is bigger than us with a great potential to stand the test of time in the history of publishing, we revised our busy schedules to make this BLUEPRINT a reality.

It's not by luck that Talifhani and I met, I believe we met by design. I've been in the game for too long. I used "books" money to pay for my school transport, trips and fees. I was selling books in High School. Any title, name it, I had it, for a good price I sold. I didn't sell a book I didn't first read, this way I learned to read faster. I still remember the night I read *Screw It, Let's Do It* by Sir. Richard Branson, I read it in front of a buyer in under 3 hours I was done. For the inconvenience, I lowered the selling price a bit, I'm a reasonable dealer.

It was inevitable for me to start a publishing company, at first, I registered a corporation back in 2013, and I had all the upcoming artists, music producers, fashion designers and writers signed in. I funded programs and events, for fashion designers I bought materials for them to cut and design in fashion shows, for DJs, I found and promoted their gigs and for writers, I published and launched their books and printed their merchandise, t-shirts, posters, caps and so on. I was everywhere doing everything.

Running this corporation was both fun and impactful, everyone knew that I'm the guy who makes things happen, I don't just talk. My name was regular in newspapers, magazines and radio stations. I was running things, nothing moved without me.

Somewhere along the way I've lost friends, made financial mistakes, experienced greedy clients, I teamed up with people who didn't wish well for me. People who were conspiring and waiting for my downfall. With the money I made from my books I would invest it in people's initiatives and dreams, this made me popular but financially I was misguided. I had a solid plan perhaps I needed backup. What I did back then helped the youth get off the street and better their lives, we were very busy, and we had a show or something every week.

I was teaching purpose and course to these youngsters. Today I'm proud of some and worried about others. I'm proud of those who carried the spirit forward, they run their own businesses today, some are married, bought houses and cars, I couldn't be prouder. Someone I was once close to in hustling is now abusing substance, he lost the drive and mojo. He goes around telling lies about me, I don't blame him for I understand the value of purpose and course, without purpose and course people perish. We move with the spirit.

I had to stop the corporation, I went to University because I love books and storytelling. On my first year, I started a film society, Cut Film Society (CFS), we nearly signed the whole class, that's how influential we were. I founded this society with friends, Aaron Rahlogo (Actor and Video Editor), Seluleko Mpisane (Director of Photography and Music Producer) and Oscar Nick (Cinematographer and Editor). I was directing the crew, we covered all TUT and regional events, our 2015 TUT Fresher's Ball prom video is running in over 10K view on YouTube.

My job was to interpret the clients brief to the crew, to provide anything needed by the crew but my favourite part was rubbing shoulders with celebrities in the VVIP and VIP sections, because I was the one creating and closing our next deals. I've seen and met every South African celebrity, in 2016 and 2017. I always told my crew that we were in the footage business. I still remember being turned down by a certain Radio station until I received their call begging for footage. I gave them a fair deal, they paid us, gave us airtime on radio to promote our movement and guaranteed us future institutional gigs. It was an exciting day for the crew. I studied the law of average from Leandri and the law of leverage from Talifhani.

Sometime in 2019 after my graduation, I had a meeting with Mr Banks in Sandton, *Slow In The City* offices to discuss business and future plans. Back at home that same day I had a dream, I woke up in the middle of the night to write what I saw. The following day I registered my company, Salmon Publishers.

As if big clients were waiting, I attracted good potential clients who wanted me to write their stories. Today I write books for medical doctors, school principals, sports stars celebrities, pastors, businessmen and politicians.

In building Salmon Publishers as a company, I had to use my earlier business experience to structure it well. I struggled with unreliable clients particularly on payments. I was operating on 'survival mode', I had to restructure my model as soon as possible. The only dispute I have with clients is mainly greedy clients trying to exploit an experienced young man.

When they email their requests for me to write their books, they write and speak in soft tones and when the book is complete, they try to play smart and speak a tough game. I don't even think this is a contract issue, I think it's our mindset as a black community, we just don't like to PAY UP, whenever it's time to pay, the tone changes. We believe because it's black, it's cheap and negotiable.

As an ordained pastor I've made a mistake of trusting people, doing handshakes and emotional agreements, this led me to so much trouble. The very same people are quick to write insults and threaten to expose you because you're a pastor. It's funny how they always jump to talk about 'exposing' me because I'm a pastor. I've learned earlier on that smaller client, those who pay a hundred bucks or five can be so much headache. Real clients who put in big money often respect me and my delivery.

I have clients who pay me a lot of money and communicate well with me even when there's a delay or a date misunderstanding, the communication is civil and respectful. Try forgetting a meeting with a client who paid you a thousand bucks, you'll see what I'm talking about, just by that alone they think you're unprofessional, you're a scam, a fly by night. All this time real clients are quite and happy with the work. Prioritize your skill and peace, it's better to take one client who's paying 100K than to take 10 clients paying 10K each. Work smart, not hard, I learnt this from Mr Banks.

> A 2-hour movie doesn't take 2 hours to
> make, so is writing a book, a 200 paged book
> like BA doesn't take 200 days to write.

Now I know not to accept any publishing or writing requests, I explain my contract before taking a project and I make my client aware that they're not the only client I have, no special treatment, only professionalism. I've developed a model that doesn't rely on client emotions but the agreed system. This method requires hard work at first but when the money starts coming in, it overflows without delay or human interference.

The secret is in the hard work, in Salmon Publishers, we focus on publishing significant stories, stories worth to be told. We are well inspired and experienced in this field. We've published a book by Mome Mahlangu, Mongezi "Tol Ass Mo" Mahlangu's wife and worked on other writing projects for the family. We've worked with Mary Ntsweng, the female soccer star in writing her book, *Striking The Balance*.

Ndivhuwo Muthivhi, a man who spent 19 years to complete his degree at University of Venda (Univen), Sontoyi Ndelema, a woman who grew up in abject poverty, brutally abused and raped but today she's a true resemblance of 'mother of the nation', she runs and supervises the Madressa Tul Umah Orphanage in Witbank, the orphanage has over 43 children. Today the Orphanage has produced graduates and successful adults.

We carefully select our authors, currently we're working on a book based on living with a disability, Dr Prudence Buthelezi is writing a book with us about her disabled sister, Thabisile Buthelezi. As the business grows, I'm becoming meticulous with the type of authors I'd love Salmon Publishers or my name to associate with.

My friendship with Mr Banks is that of a brother and friend, I don't claim to know him better than anyone else, but I've been with him enough to tell his story. Through him, I got clients and referrals, he's that helpful and powerful. There were days of course where he needed my help, mostly as a pastor and I would gladly offer that to him, prayers and counsel. Above all, we survived and pulled through.

Writing a killer book has always been my dream; the only problem was the materialization of its possibility. The fact that something is possible does not necessarily mean it'll happen unless if you ensure its occurrence. Ensuring that your dream becomes a reality requires more than just the talking and the dreaming process. Albert Einstein believed that any intelligent fool could make things bigger and more complex... it takes a touch a touch of genius - and a lot of courage to move in the opposite direction.

I have no doubt that SALOM PUBLISHERS is a publishing giant, I'm combining all my skills and qualifications to develop one of the best publishing corporations that will touch on all forms of storytelling, broadcasting, writing and filming. This year we're expanding and opening an office in the East of Pretoria. I'm in the energy business, I prefer positive energy dealings and relationships. This is beyond my ambition.

I dreamt of a salmon fish swimming against tides like an eagle in the storm. I woke up to learn that this fish resembles determination, courage and resilience. These attributes described me, I hustle smart, I never give up; won't stop, can't stop, WE'RE GOING UPSTREAM!

"

Having lived in informal settlements for more than a decade, I realized that the world doesn't come to a standstill because you're unemployed and nor does your country under-develop because you failed to develop".

"

I didn't want to be employed

or

anything, I just wanted to graduate.

"

A 2-hour movie doesn't take 2 hours to make, so is writing a book, a 200 paged book like BA doesn't take 200 days to write

"

Real clients who put in big money understand professionalism and etiquette.

12.

GOD

Is

King

We're representing the higher source of energy that's beyond us and connecting us to create and invent. This wall symbolizes the beauty and power of the Almighty and we are living up to it. As a collaborative of creators, great inventors and pioneers in the data technology there should be something powerful of a higher power connecting us.

This is words from my heart, I became great the day I started embracing giving, I give without expecting anything to be honest. I have given my skills, knowledge and jobs to many people. One thing I always notice is everyone who get to work with me or get close to me for some time, get to realise their potential.

Some people won't tell you how their lives have changed through my connection but instead they might tell you how I am not helping them as I become more successful.

I had already developed a strategic listening skill. I attentively listen to someone and still understand that their limited knowledge of vision is making them to think like that. The main reason behind 'God is King' wall in our office is beyond just praising and acknowledging the Higher Power but more so a proclamation that this is a home of "creators". In Analytics Advertising, We Create!

God representing the higher source of energy that is beyond us and connecting us together to create and invent. It turns out so many people connected with the wall overtime and when they come to the Data Valley they always want to take a picture on the wall. The God is King wall is becoming a representation of greatness and faith towards each one's ambitions.

We became a representation of hope in Africa as a Data Tech company and this is what we are doing it for, to remind each other that through faith it can be done and that's how you creatively create.

They're not taught on how to create through faith, and they don't understand but if you listen to them long enough you will start to believe and think they are right. They talk as if they know but they haven't created anything, they only criticize. You might also find them criticizing this book that is meant to help them transform.

We sold more than 4000 copies on this book on our first version in 2019. We were testing if the market will understand, people transformed and that's where we knew we need to add more chapters to make it a blueprint for the community across Africa. We received powerful testimonials and feedback from our customers.

It was not a mistake to collaborate with our best ordained pastor "Pastor Kika" to help me write this book, this is a spiritual book, it has the ability to transform you to a beast that you are. How to turn into an award-winning company or person, how to unleash your full potential, how to become a leading publisher or someone with a calculus mind like

Talifhani, the book gives answers and solutions to your questions and problems.

This book represents the glory of higher power and how God is King. We trust you'll find out how we creatively applied faith and became a success story, Beyond Ambition.

Truthfully, it was not easy when we started, a lot of people didn't understand what we were doing. It's only now after years of hard and smart work is everything coming and working together, it all makes sense now, suddenly everyone is proud of what we have accomplished. It's amazing how God will take you through situations that you never thought you will be able to come out from, God is King indeed!

Ignore the naysayers, we wouldn't be here if we'd listen to all the negative and evil voices, we pushed the work regardless. If you're going to set your company or life in such a way that offers solutions and answers to the market, you've got to thoroughly understand problems and questions.

Don't wish it were easy, wish you were better, don't wish for less problems, wish for more skills.

-Jim Rohn

To become a disruptor and a visionary leader, you ought to work on 5 keys:

1. Transform your mind
2. Have drive
3. Be Patient
4. You will hit your luck
5. Be consistent

All rejections are redirections, don't take anything personal, Let's Work!

Analytics Advertising is growing both hyperbolically and exponentially. Every growth means 3 times more growth within a short span of time and we have learned to leverage this.

5 years from now will be amazing, we will be working internationally partnering with large corporations and standing out as a modern, large Data Tech consulting firm.

As I finish this book, I have been invited to speak at the "Global 2020 Expo" In Dubai now in March 2022 about how we are using technology, Innovations and AI to creatively help global corporations to be sustainable.

It is not a secret anymore that we are a number one Data Tech company in the medium enterprise In **Africa**.

In this case, we didn't go to the Mountain and came back different, we've left the blueprint throughout the book. There's no magic, snake or funny business, we went through the process.

We've started from the bottom and now we are HERE!

The future is bright, and God bless you.

God is King!

In Analytics Advertising, We Create!

"

Ignore the naysayers, we wouldn't be here if we'd listen to all the negative and evil voices, we pushed the work regardless.

"

If you're going to set your company or life in such a way that offers solutions and answers to the market, you've got to thoroughly understand problems and questions.

NOTES

BEYOND AMBITION

BEYOND AMBITION

9 780620 852944